T0419567

ADVANCES IN SOCIOLOGY RESEARCH

VOLUME 29

ADVANCES IN SOCIOLOGY RESEARCH

ADVANCES IN SOCIOLOGY RESEARCH

VOLUME 29

JARED A. JAWORSKI
EDITOR

nova
science publishers
New York

NOTICE TO THE READER

Library of Congress Cataloging-in-Publication Data

ISBN: 978-1-53616-781-8
ISSN: 1558-0385

Published by Nova Science Publishers, Inc. † New York

CONTENTS

PREFACE

Advances in Sociology Research. Volume 29 first presents a critical review of the major theoretical approaches to the study of voluntary homicide. One such group of theories refers to the so-called structural perspective, which argues that the killing of one person by another must be interpreted in the broader context of the social structure. Another group of theories refers to culture whereas some people engage in homicides mainly because they hold facilitative attitudes or values transmitted by their subcultures. Lastly, the chapter devotes space to the theories referring to the symbolic interactionist approach, which emphasizes the importance of the interaction between the perpetrator and victim of homicides.

Next, the first research findings of the EU funded project Local Alliance for Integration in the field of healthcare and social care at a national level are presented, drawing upon the empirical findings of one focus group with local stakeholders in the field of healthcare and social care.

Additionally, cyberbullying through social media among youth is examined through multidisciplinary qualitative, quantitative, and mixed-design research methodologies from psychology, sociology, social work, and criminology.

The authors describe a project set up in East London that assessed the use of music technology as one of the primary tools in an extra-curricular music programmes, and outline its primary findings with specific reference to its potential effect on children's social behaviours.

Online risks children may encounter are examined, including content risk such as online video games and contact risk related to sexting and sexual solicitation. The importance of awareness and education is emphasised along with future directions to ensure children are protected while participating in the online space.

The penultimate chapter looks at how the greater part of female models are being shown in agreeable, subordinate and sexualized ways using nude, half-clad appearances of men and women. The unrealistic image portrayals in these advertisements could be inherently dangerous.

The closing article discusses dilemmas of understanding the individual, presented through a scene from Monty Python's Life of Brian. The speech which Brian delivers to his assembled followers and the reactions to it display typical conceptual problems arising in both the Enlightenment's "ideology of individualism" and its arguable follow-up, the Romantic favoring of "individuality".

Chapter 1 - Theoretical and empirical work focusing on criminal behaviors has a long history in sociology, and has also been carried out by some of the discipline's classic authors. A significant place in this large body of knowledge is occupied by the strands of research devoted to understanding voluntary homicide, universally recognized across time and cultures to be one of the most serious kinds of deviant behavior. In the field of social sciences, much work has been done on this topic, particularly in the United States, where lethal violence is more widespread than in most Western countries. This chapter offers a critical review of the major theoretical approaches to the study of voluntary homicide. One group of theories refers to the so-called structural perspective, which argues that the killing of one person by another is not simply an individual act of violence, but must be interpreted in the broader context of the social structure, i.e., the social positions individuals occupy and the behavioral expectations attached to them. Another group of theories refers to culture, which together with social structure is one of the two pillars of social organization. In this view, some people engage in homicides mainly because they hold facilitative attitudes or values that the subculture in which they have been socialized attaches to this deviant behavior. Lastly, the chapter devotes space to the theories referring to the symbolic interactionist approach, which emphasizes the importance of the interaction between the perpetrator and victim of homicides, as well as the role of the interpretations of social experiences whereby people develop a favorable attitude toward the use of lethal violence. The chapter concludes with some considerations underscoring the importance of combining these approaches in order to fully understand the phenomenon of voluntary homicide.

Chapter 2 - Since 2015, the European continent confronts an unprecedented migration influx that has triggered humanitarian crisis. Years later, the first waves of uprooted populations are seeking integration in the host countries, while Greece is setting up viable national strategies so as to integrate Third Country Nationals (TCNs). This chapter presents the first research findings of the EU funded project *Local Alliance for Integration* (accr. LION) in the field of healthcare and social care at a national level. It draws upon the empirical findings of one focus group with local stakeholders in the field of healthcare and social care in order to address the needs of TCNs and reveals the existing challenges. The qualitative research took place in Athens and centres around the integration policies in the field of healthcare and social care under the methodological prism and review of best practices at EU and national level (Greece). It is argued that there are still some measures to be taken in order to cover adequately the healthcare and social care needs of TCNs, such as intercultural mediation and interpreting in the Greek National Health System (NHS); information provision regarding the healthcare rights of the newcomers; strengthening the housing policy and maintaining funds for vulnerable groups such as unaccompanied minors, victims of torture, Gender-Based Violence (GBV) and Sexual and Gender-Based Violence (SGBV) survivors; a well-designed integration plan at a national level; and stronger coordination between the Greek State and non-state organisations. In conclusion, even though the crisis days are past behind us, the country - in many parts - is still struggling at the level of emergency.

Chapter 3 - The purpose of this chapter is to examine cyberbullying through social media among youth. An extension of traditional bullying, cyberbullying is a form of bullying which takes place by means of electronic technologies, such as email, instant messaging, social media, and text messaging through mobile devices. Drawing on research from a variety of disciplines, such as psychology, education, social work, sociology, and computer science, this chapter is organized into six sections. These sections include: (1) explaining the definitions, technologies used, the role of anonymity, and prevalence rates of cyberbullying, (2) discussing the characteristics and risk factors associated with cyberbullying involvement, (3) reviewing research findings on the psychosocial and behavioral consequences resulting from cyberbullying involvement, (4) discussing strategies to prevent cyberbullying and recommendations, (5) explaining future research directions, and (6) closing remarks about cyberbullying. The chapter draws on multidisciplinary qualitative, quantitative, and mixed-design research methodologies.

Chapter 4 - A considerable amount of research has been conducted on different art forms and their possible effect on social behaviours. Such research has broadened the authors' understanding of social behaviours and human nature. For instance, group music-making activities have been linked to enhanced ability to communicate. Currently, with the increasing use of music technology in education, there has been debate on the potential impact of technology on children's social behaviours. In order to investigate the issue further, a project was set up in East London (UK) that assessed the use of music technology as one of the primary tools in an extra-curricularmusic programme consisting of collaborative and individual music-making activities. In this chapter, the authors will describe the project in detail and outline its primary findings, with specific reference to its potential effect on children's social behaviours. The social context of the project is considered and how similar projects could potentially be implemented in other contexts.

Chapter 5 - Online technologies have changed the lives of children and their families. They create countless benefits including for education, health, recreation and connecting people in removing physical barriers.

However, these new ways of social networking bring with them unique risks. Women are uniquely positioned as gatekeepers to protect children from sexual exploitation and other forms of victimisation. This chapter examines online risks children may encounter including *content risk* such as online video games and *contact risk* related to sexting and sexual solicitation. The importance of awareness and education is emphasised along with future directions to ensure children are protected while participating in the online space.

Chapter 6 - Online technologies have changed the lives of children and their families. They create countless benefits including for education, health, recreation and connecting people in removing physical barriers. However, these new ways of social networking bring with them unique risks. Women are uniquely positioned as gatekeepers to protect children from sexual exploitation and other forms of victimisation. This chapter examines online risks children may encounter including *content risk* such as online video games and *contact risk* related to sexting and sexual solicitation. The importance of awareness and education is emphasised along with future directions to ensure children are protected while participating in the online space.

Chapter 7 - The article discusses dilemmas of understing the individual, which are presented through a scene from *Monty Python's Life of Brian*. The speech which Brian delievers to his assembled followers and the reactions to it amusingly display typical conceptual problems arising in both the Englightment's 'ideology of individualism' – which claims that the individual is opposed to the collective and above it – and its arguable follow-up, the Romantic favorizing of 'individuality'. Special attention is given to the dynamic journey of both imposing and expanding the individuality of a single personality, to the point of having it 'swallowed up' in supra-personal entities. The conclusion suggests that contemporary understandings of the 'individual' have shifted from 'final indivisibility' to negation of every subsummation, including the one that affirms it, at the price of a paradox that bears witness to its fragile theoretical construction.

In: Advances in Sociology Research   ISBN: 978-1-53616-781-8
Editor: Jared A. Jaworski   © 2020 Nova Science Publishers, Inc.

Chapter 1

THEORETICAL SOCIOLOGICAL PERSPECTIVES EXPLAINING LETHAL VIOLENCE: A MATTER OF STRUCTURE, CULTURE OR INTERPERSONAL INTERACTIONS?

Lorenzo Todesco

University of Torino, Department of Cultures, Politics and Society,
Lungo Dora Siena, 100, 10153 Torino (Italy)

ABSTRACT

Theoretical and empirical work focusing on criminal behaviors has a long history in sociology, and has also been carried out by some of the discipline's classic authors. A significant place in this large body of knowledge is occupied by the strands of research devoted to understanding voluntary homicide, universally recognized across time and cultures to be one of the most serious kinds of deviant behavior. In the field of social sciences, much work has been done on this topic, particularly in the United States, where lethal violence is more widespread than in most Western countries. This chapter offers a critical review of the major theoretical approaches to the study of voluntary homicide. One group of theories refers to the so-called structural perspective, which argues that the killing of one person by another is not simply an individual act of violence, but must be interpreted in the broader context of the social structure, i.e., the social positions individuals occupy and the behavioral expectations attached to them. Another group of theories refers to culture, which together with social structure is one of the two pillars of social organization. In this view, some people engage in homicides mainly because they hold facilitative attitudes or values that the subculture in which they have been socialized attaches to this deviant behavior. Lastly, the chapter devotes space to the theories referring to the symbolic interactionist approach, which emphasizes the importance of the interaction between the perpetrator and victim of homicides, as well as the role of the interpretations of social experiences whereby people develop a favorable attitude toward the use of lethal violence. The chapter concludes with some considerations underscoring the importance of combining these approaches in order to fully understand the phenomenon of voluntary homicide.

INTRODUCTION

Sociology has made a major contribution to the development of criminology (Rock, 2002), with theories devised to explain deviant and criminal behaviors, of which homicide is universally recognized to be one of the worst forms. Sociology's contributions in this area began between the mid-1920s and the early '30s in the United States, with the work of the Chicago School (see, for example, Park, Burgess, & McKenzie, 1925), and received a further impetus at the end of the '30s, when Robert K. Merton (1938) built on the thinking of Emile Durkheim (1897) and Thorsten Sellin (1938). New theoretical work stemming from an entirely different approach was produced in the '60s (H. S. Becker, 1963; Kitsuse & Cicourel, 1963) and, more recently, in the mid-90s (Milovanovic, 1996, 1997).

This chapter will not review all of sociology's attempts to explain deviance and criminality on a theoretical basis in the course of nearly a century. Rather, it will present a critical appraisal of the approaches that have most frequently been employed to shed light on the dynamics that generate extreme violence: violence resulting in the killing of one or more human beings. Most of these attempts at explanation draw on sociology's three classic theoretical perspectives: the structuralist, the culturalist and the interactionist. These perspectives are often regarded as highly dissimilar – if not indeed in open opposition – to each other. Nevertheless, each contributes to explaining a different aspect of homicide, a multi-faceted phenomenon which, as we will see, spans the macro and micro dimensions. It must also be borne in mind that the term homicide covers an extremely wide range of episodes of lethal violence: from those that are purely instrumental in intent – with a clear goal and a rational motive, often linked to economic considerations – to those that are referred to as expressive, where the murderer has often failed to calculate the costs and benefits in any way. Through killing, in fact, murderers manifest their state of mind, their uncontrolled impulses and their emotions. In the following pages, we will see how different theories can be used case by case to illuminate the distinctive dynamic of one kind of homicide rather than another.

The structuralist and culturalist approaches seek to explain the different murder rates among different populations – or in the same population as it changes over time – adopting comparative and diachronic methods. In explaining the different models of lethal violence, these perspectives focus on certain characteristics of the killer (and sometimes of the victim as well) and of their social context. Accordingly, they investigate how certain macro – or, in rarer cases, meso-level factors – poverty, for example, inequality or a value system held by a subculture such as a neighborhood youth gang – can influence the incidence of different kinds of homicide. The structuralist perspective seems particularly effective in casting light on episodes of instrumental lethal violence, though some of its adherents have attempted to broaden its focus to include other types of homicide. By contrast, the culturalist perspective can explain certain instrumental homicides – in terms, for instance, of a form of social redemption – as effectively as it explains more expressive lethal events: such as those, as we will see, associated at the symbolic level with territorial control, or with affirming one's honor, courage or masculinity.

The interactionist approach – as the name suggests – puts the accent on the interactional dynamics between murderers, their victims and any witnesses, on their spatial and social contexts, and on interpreting the social experiences that can work together in generating brutal and violent behavior. Here, attention centers on the chain of interactions that lead to killing a person, essentially ignoring murder's incidence at the macro level and the dynamics that influence it. The interactionist perspective is particularly important for understanding expressive homicides, including those involving people who know each other intimately, those involving acquaintances or strangers, and those occurring for seemingly trivial motives.

As we will argue in the concluding pages of this chapter, triangulating these three perspectives can provide a fuller picture of the contexts and dynamics underlying a phenomenon as multidimensional, complex and heterogeneous as homicide.

THE STRUCTURALIST PERSPECTIVE

The origins of the structuralist perspective date to the 1930s. Modified and revised, it is still widely used today. Its basic assumption is that homicide is not a simple act of isolated violence triggered by the interaction between the killer and the victim; rather, it is – in Durkheimian terms – a "social fact", which depends to a large extent on the social structure and context in which it takes place (Messner & Rosenfeld, 1999). Starting from this assumption, what dimensions of homicide and what kinds of lethal episode can this approach explain? Structuralist theoreticians take a macro-level view of homicide. Consequently, they are not interested in the interpersonal dynamics whereby a social interaction can end in a killing, nor in the social processes that lead an individual to kill. Rather, they want to understand what elements of the social context influence the homicide rates in different areas or in the same area at different points in time. In the case of the United States, for example, researchers have put considerable effort into explaining why murder rates in the South are much higher than in other parts of the country (the so-called "South versus West Debate", see Brookman, 2005; Beeghley, 2003). Attention focuses not only on the social context, but on the individual characteristics that, taken together, create it. Are there social classes, ethnic groups and age groups where homicide is more frequent? Are there gender differences in the incidence of lethal violence? If such variability exists, what dynamics explain it?

The structuralist perspective is closely concerned with the role that deprivation plays in the development of criminal behaviors such as homicide. At first glance, then, this approach would appear to be most suitable for understanding instrumental homicides. And to some extent this is true, though as we will see, a number of scholars taking this perspective have sought to extend it to other types of homicide. Despite this laudable effort, however, instrumental episodes still appear to be this approach's main purview.

Before going into the details of the structuralist view of homicide, a few words are in order concerning several basic notions. Social structure – together with culture – is one of the two pillars of social organization: it describes the enduring and patterned network of relationships between the components of social reality, which create a system of opportunities and constraints around the social actors. One of the fundamental features of the social structure are the different positions – called roles – that individuals occupy (a person can, for example, be a co-worker, son, fiancé, neighbor and so forth), each of which carries a set of expectations and obligations.

Alongside roles, the second component of the social structure are the institutions, which are of particular importance given their link to the realm of values. Institutions are relatively stable configurations of statuses, roles, values and norms that are essential to society's basic functioning because they satisfy specific social needs (Messner & Rosenfeld, 1999). Examples of institutions include the economy, which deals with the production and distribution of goods and services; the political system, which distributes power among social groups, mobilizes resources and organizes action for collective goal attainment; and the family, which socializes new members of society in its values and beliefs. Institutions are at the foundation of society, as they are rooted in the social structure and support its culture and values. Explanations of social behavior based on roles and the expectations attached to them are referred to as "structural", precisely because they are relatively stable and enduring characteristics of social reality.

Independently of the aims of their action, all institutions share two basic functions: regulating members' behavior so that it is in line with the society's normative patterns, and facilitating members' access to the system of resources and rewards (Messner & Rosenfeld, 1999). These two functions are especially prominent in some of the best-known structuralist theories of homicide: the first function informs theory linking homicide and the erosion of social control (social disorganization theory, social control theory), while the second underlies theories that link homicidal violence to increases in social strain (strain theory). These theories stem from the broader absence or deficit paradigm, which traces the causes of deviance and criminality to various kinds of social, economic and cultural failure (Prina, 2019).

One characteristic of the social structure that is very important for an understanding of the reasons that bring a person to kill is social stratification: the hierarchical system that establishes relatively stable rankings for each individual, with statuses that can vary widely in wealth, power or prestige. As social stratification is based on social class, race, gender and age, these characteristics – together with other macro-level characteristics that will be discussed later – are also of particular interest in homicide studies. As we will see, the adherents of the structuralist approach argue that structural social inequalities, such as deprivation or the lack of opportunities, set the scene for lethal violence.

Social Disorganization Theory

Social disorganization theory was originally put forward by several members of the Chicago School (for two classic treatments, see Park et al., 1925; Thomas & Znaniecki, 1920). This school's approaches to investigating criminal behavior have varied widely both at the theoretical level – ranging from symbolic interactionism (Anderson, 1923) and the culture-conflict hypothesis (Wirth, 1931), to the so-called ecological model (see below) – and from the methodological standpoint, where everything from official statistics to ethnographic methods has been used. What is distinctive of the Chicago School, however, is its emphasis on community, where the community can be a city, a neighborhood, an ethnic group, a marginal community, and so forth.

The ecological model occupies a prime position among structuralist theories explaining homicide rates. According to this model, this serious crime, like delinquent behaviors in general, can only be understood by investigating how individuals move in their natural environment – in their space and in their time – just as botanists and zoologists do with plants and animals (Williams & McShane, 1994). From this standpoint, it is necessary to focus on the macro-level elements that weaken the social control that their communities exercise on individuals: the environment, in fact, has a significant impact on the actors' actions (Messner & Rosenfeld, 1999).

The social disorganization approach holds that primary social relationships can be weakened in large cities (Williams & McShane, 1994). This draws on Durkheim's concept of anomie (1897): the breakdown of the shared constellation of values resulting in a lack of clear norms indicating which behaviors should be embraced and which should be avoided. Here, the concept of anomie is applied to the living conditions of some segments of the population in certain urban areas; anomie is what generates a favorable setting for homicidal violence, even though it is subject to stringent norms and sanctions in all societies.

Primary social relationships are likely to weaken in areas where most individuals are unknown to each other and bonds between family, friends and neighbors are loose. This breaks apart the community's relational fabric, meaning that the residents of a given urban area are unable to live together cooperatively, so that there are few strong formal and informal associational ties. This disorganization saps the social control that under normal circumstances contributes to curbing homicides and criminality in general (Bursik JR., 1988; Shaw & McKay, 1942): this process of demoralization is at the basis of social pathologies such as alcoholism, homelessness, prostitution and the various forms of criminal behavior.

Social disorganization is caused by macro-level factors, where migratory flows play an important role: continual population turnover can produce a local community which has no solid relationships or shared constellation of values, as it is unable to maintain effective social control in its area. In addition, residential mobility makes it difficult to identify with the neighborhood, and there is a tendency to try to escape from it as soon as possible. Newly arrived immigrants – finding themselves in an unknown environment – withdraw into their culture of origin, triggering a conflict with the dominant culture that aggravates the effects of social disorganization. This type of community is dominated by territorial tensions and conflicts that bring about a significant increase in crime rates and, consequently, produce fertile ground for homicides. Other factors in addition to population turnover also contribute to social disorganization: economic deprivation, ethnic heterogeneity and family disruption, with large numbers of disadvantaged or broken families (Sampson & Groves, 1989). Yet another factor is the degree of urban decay shown by a given area (Shaw & McKay, 1942).

As mentioned earlier, the social disorganization approach originated with studies carried out in Chicago during the 1920s (Burgess, 1925; Park et al., 1925). At the time, the downtown area was the business district, occupied chiefly by factories and office buildings, but with few residences. Next to it was the so-called zone of transition, where factors and businesses were encroaching, making it less than desirable as a location for residences. This, however, made it the cheapest place to live, and so immigrants settled there, attracted to the area because it was inexpensive and close to the factories where they hoped to find jobs. As soon as they could afford it, though, they moved to the next zone, less decayed but farther from the center: the zone of workingmen's homes. They were replaced in the zone of transition by the next waves of immigrants. Beyond the workingmen's zone, towards the outskirts of the city, lay the middle- and upper-class residential zone. Radiating out from the center, then, the city's zones were increasingly more prestigious, and more expensive to live in (Williams & McShane, 1994).

Crime rates in these zones of Chicago during the Twenties differed widely according to their level of social disorganization: homicides and delinquency – as well as tuberculosis, infant mortality, mental health problems and alcoholism – were most frequent in the zone of transition, and became progressively less frequent moving from the center outwards (Shaw, 1929; Shaw & McKay, 1942). The most interesting point here is that this held true independently of the individuals living in each zone: the differences in crime rate between these areas remained virtually constant throughout the first two decades of the twentieth century, even as the population and its ethnic makeup was in constant flux (Shaw, 1929; Shaw & McKay, 1942). This shows that violence and homicides do not depend so much on the characteristics of the individual social actors, as they do how individual actions are affected by the social structure: in this case, the local community's level of integration and social organization. According to Shaw and McKay's cultural transmission theory (1942), young people and newcomers living in a socially disorganized area have a high likelihood of coming into contact with violence and criminal elements. These areas thus develop what can only be regarded as a delinquent tradition, whose values and behaviors – including homicide – are handed down from generation to generation, just like language or other aspects of social life. This is why Robert Park wrote of a true "social contagion" among the inhabitants of the same area of a city, who develop common life styles and values, reinforcing and justifying each other's conduct (Prina, 2019)

Social Control Theory

A number of versions of social control theory have been put forward by American scholars (Nye, 1958; Reckless, 1955; Reiss, 1951; Toby, 1957) since the 1950s. The version that has gained the most ground is that advanced by Travis Hirschi (1969; see also Sampson & Laub, 1993), the so-called bonding theory. The core idea of Hirschi's thinking – shared by other social control theorists – is that people are essentially selfish by nature, and consequently seek to achieve their aims by any means, lawful or unlawful. In some situations, then, social actors can even go so far as to kill, if this action brings them advantages they would not gain if they were to let their victim live. It should be emphasized that it is advisable to consider not only the economic and tangible advantages that can accrue from killing someone, even though they are undeniably important in this theoretical framework. In addition, the symbolic benefits in terms of authority or identity should also be borne in mind in order to extend the range of homicide situations that this approach can explain.

According to social control theorists, the role of the social structure and institutions is to limit the actors' selfish interests, constraining them and encouraging the actors to live together in the most civil and peaceful way possible. But if the structure and the institutions lose strength, there will be more frequent instances of individualistic behavior, including episodes of violence. This approach has a great deal in common with the Chicago School's social disorganization theory: Hirschi, in fact, stated expressly (see Bartollas, 1985) that the disorganization approach is at the basis of the social control approach. However, while the former focuses on the effects of the lack of social control at the community level, the latter puts greater stress on individuals (Messner & Rosenfeld, 1999).

Social control theory seeks to cast light on the concept of social bond, positing four micro-level elements of bond that contribute to people's natural tendency to infringe norms: attachment, involvement, commitment and belief (Hirschi, 1969; see also Williams & McShane, 1994). The most important of these is attachment – the affective dimension of the social bond – both to significant others (family members, friends and so on), and to institutions (school, associations, etc.); attachment is at the basis of compliance with social norms, even when significant others engage in deviant behavior.

Involvement is the time dimension of the social bond, and refers to the time and energy that individuals devote to their activities, both those that are in line with conventional society, and those that diverge from them. As involvement in socially accepted activities increases, so does the individual's level of conformity, as there is less time and energy available for deviant behavior. This is an idea that has a firm grip on the popular imagination, as demonstrated by the old saying "the Devil finds work for idle hands": people with too much spare time risk infringing the norms more than those with a full social life (Barbagli, Colombo, & Savona, 2003).

Commitment is the material dimension of the social bond: the investments that a person makes in the various areas of conventional society, such as education, employment, reputation. People with years of schooling that have enabled them to embark on a prestigious career, working their way up through the ranks, will be less likely to kill than an uneducated person who gets by day by day, living from hand to mouth. The latter, in fact, has less to lose if he is found guilty of such a serious crime, and one that carries lengthy prison terms that nullify extensive commitment and investments made in conventional society. There is thus a fear of the costs that homicide entails, which varies considerably from individual to individual.

Lastly, belief is associated with the moral dimension of the social bond, or the validity that the actors assign to social norms: the more the norms are believed to be valid, part of a moral obligation arising from the shared constellation of values, the less the likelihood of engaging in deviant and criminal behavior.

These four elements, then, reinforce or weaken the bond that each individual has with society, and hence the choice of committing an act as fraught with consequences as homicide. And these elements are all correlated with each other: if one loses strength, sooner or later the others will too, one after another. In turn, the social structure, its institutions and the system of structural inequalities influence these elements: economic vulnerability, for example, jeopardizes individuals' educational careers, thus complicating their attachment, involvement and commitment to schooling. Family disruption puts attachment to other family members at risk, just as population turnover and heterogeneity can be detrimental to neighborhood relationships, further reducing attachment to significant others.

Strain Theory

Strain theory was first formalized by Robert K. Merton in "Social Structure and Anomie" (1938), starting from a reformulation of the Durkheimian concept of anomie discussed above. This theory – which was taken up again and extended in later years (see, for instance, Agnew, 1992; Cloward & Ohlin, 1960; Cohen, 1955)[*] – deals with the role institutions play in facilitating people's access to the material, social and symbolic resources needed, not only for mere survival, but also for the full enjoyment of social citizenship: as famously defined by Marshall (1950), the whole range from the right to a modicum of economic welfare and security to the right to share to the full in the social heritage and to live the life of a civilized being according to the standards prevailing in the society.

Merton argues that relative deprivation is crucial to understanding criminal behaviors: not deprivation in absolute terms – or deprivation *per se* – but deprivation which is perceived as such by comparison with some unattainable standard[†].

Institutions regulate individuals' access to prestige, power and wealth, thus determining their actual life chances (Messner & Rosenfeld, 1999). According to strain theory, crime and violence – including that resulting in a killing – are linked to certain structural conditions (Cohen, 1955): primarily, differences in social origin and the unequal distribution of access to education and the better jobs. These conditions make it very difficult if not impossible for some people to obtain the resources, rewards and prestige they need, expect or feel entitled to because conventional society regards them as desirable. Merton (1938) thus reformulates

---

[*] We will discuss the contributions made by Cohen and by Cloward and Ohlin later, in the section on subcultural theories. These scholars, in fact, sought to combine a culturalist approach to criminality with Merton's strain theory.

[†] On the relationship between relative deprivation and absolute deprivation and their effects on homicide counts, see the recent empirical study by Burraston and colleagues (2019).

Durkheim's concept of anomie as the situation in which society lays down the aims that people should aspire to – putting more emphasis on some than on others – and the legitimate means for obtaining them, without, however, providing all actors with the actual opportunities for doing so lawfully. This, then, sets up a strain – hence the name of the theory – between the cultural structure, or in other words the institutionalized goals and means, and the social structure: how opportunities for success are distributed according to the status accorded to each actor's role. A socially pathological situation arises when goals are highly emphasized, but less importance is assigned – especially during the socialization process – to using lawful means and rejecting unlawful ones.

According to Merton (1938), the anomie resulting from the strain between the social structure and the cultural structure is what induces certain individuals to commit crimes: the constraints on the opportunities for self-realization generate frustration, and are potential catalysts for episodes of violence, including lethal ones. Like all structuralist approaches, the strain approach thus focuses on analyzing the social structure's function in creating deviance, without specifying the processes located at the micro level that lead individual actors to depart from the norms of conventional society.

The social classes that run the greatest risk of turning to criminal behavior are the deprived segments, who experience the anomie that results when the opportunities available to them consistently fall short of their aspirations. There is also a further element that contributes to criminality: lawful means are not necessarily the most efficient ways of reaching socially prescribed goals. For a lower class actor with few opportunities for social betterment, robbing a bank may be a far more efficient way of improving his economic status than honest toil (Williams & McShane, 1994). As this example illustrates, strain theory is particularly useful for shedding light on instrumental homicides, which can contribute to narrowing the gap separating cultural structure and social structure, as in the case of homicides committed in the course of other predatory crimes. As we will see in a moment, however, the lethal episodes that can be explained by this theory are in fact far more varied.

According to Merton (1938), the strain between cultural goals, institutionalized means and social structure generates four models of deviant behavior, three of which are of particular interest to us here, as they help illuminate the reasons that can lead to the killing of a fellow human being. First, we have the people, whom Merton calls innovators, who accept the socially prescribed goals but are willing to employ unlawful means to reach them, and may even kill in the process: this is the case, for instance, of instrumental killings during robberies staged by organized crime.

The second type of deviant behavior is called retreatism, a term referring to the rejection of both goals and means, and applied to people who live at the margins of society, like vagrants, chronic drunks and drug addicts. In this case, lethal violence can be a rash act resulting from substance abuse – and thus not classifiable as either instrumental or entirely expressive – or from the need (in which case it is indeed instrumental) to get money quickly and at all costs to pay for the habit.

Lastly, we have the rebels: people who reject both the prescribed goals and the accepted means, but replace them with other goals and other means. This model of behavior is particularly important in understanding forms of homicide associated with political terrorism or religious extremism[*].

It must be emphasized that the socially prescribed goals have long been identified – starting in the United States, where this theory was first developed – with access to wealth and material wellbeing. In this way, however, the strain approach can help us understand only those lethal encounters where the offender gains some financial benefit from the murder (Brookman, 2005). Thus, as noted earlier, this approach would seem to be of little use in explaining many different kinds of killing, such as crimes of passion and those escalating from quarrels or motivated by revenge. Over time, strain theory has been revised and extended, and the

---

[*] Merton's fourth model of deviant behavior, which he calls ritualism, is not pertinent to an understanding of homicide. Ritualists reject socially accepted goals, but abide by the institutionalized means. This behavior is deviant in that it departs from society's dominant values and does not contribute to its functioning, but does not risk ending in criminal and violent conduct. An example of a ritualist would be someone who works hard for his own security, but not in order to gain wealth.

positively valued goals are no longer limited to the sphere of material wellbeing, but also involve dimensions such as independence, authority and identity (see, for example, Agnew, 1992, 2001; Elliott, Ageton, & Canter, 1979)*. An interesting example is that of femicide, the extreme means used by male perpetrators to affirm their gender identity and impose their conception of male authority on their female victims (see, for example, Radford & Russell, 1992). This extension of the theory significantly increases the number of cases of homicide that the strain approach can effectively explain.

THE CULTURALIST PERSPECTIVE

The origins of the culturalist approach date to the same period as those of the structuralist approach, and are to be found in the work of Thorsten Sellin in the late 1930s (Sellin, 1938). What elements of homicide – which as we have said is a complex, multidimensional phenomenon – can this perspective explain more effectively than the structuralist approach? It goes without saying that *not* all actors who find themselves in a position of severe social deprivation, or who live in a socially disorganized setting, get to the point of killing another person. The culturalist approach seeks to shed light precisely on why actors behave differently even when their circumstances are structurally similar. In other words, it attempts to understand why certain individuals kill and others do not, despite having similar sociodemographic characteristics, occupying the same position in the social inequality pyramid and being in the same macro-context (Corzine, Huff-Corzine, & Whitt, 1999). From the standpoint of the culturalist approach, it is because social actions are not governed only by the structure, but also by individuals' value constellation and the norms that guide them. These factors can vary – and quite widely – even among subjects with similar structural characteristics, in some cases producing a

---

* It should, however, be noted that Merton himself cited economic success as an emblematic example, but not the only important goal recognized by the American society of his day (Williams & McShane, 1994).

true subculture of violence that justifies criminal behavior. While structuralist theories focus on the social conditions that can drive a person to kill, their culturalist counterparts unpack the values and norms that make an action acceptable that is generally seen as seriously deviant. They thus contribute to explaining an important element of homicide.

From its beginnings, the culturalist perspective has been used to understand a wider range of killings than the structuralist approach. It is undoubtedly useful for casting light on instrumental homicides, which it regards as a sort of proving ground for a subculture of individuals who are unable – because of their social origin – to improve their status by following the rules of conventional society. In addition, it can also be applied to some expressive homicides, viz., those arising out of an exaggerated expression of honor, courage or manliness. Examples range from homicides between members of rival gangs defending their territory – for reasons that are symbolic as well as economic – to those resulting from an altercation that has got out of hand between people who know each other or are total strangers, and to femicides where a man kills a woman who has announced her decision to leave him or rejects his advances.

According to Corzine and colleagues (1999), the most useful conceptualization of how different value constellations affect the decision to engage in violent behavior is Swidler's (1986) idea of culture as a "tool kit" of symbols, stories, rituals and world-views which social actors use in varying ways to provide them with guidance in dealing with everyday decisions. To analyze culture's effects on social reality, it is thus necessary to focus on people's strategies of action, or in other words their relatively persistent ways of acting through time; in fact, culture exerts its effect not only in defining ends of actions, but also in providing cultural components that are used to construct strategies of action (Swidler, 1986).

Essentially, culture as a tool kit influences levels of criminal and violent behavior – including those with fatal outcome – in two ways (Corzine et al., 1999). First, there is a culture associated with the use and knowledge of weapons: while everyone can see that a large stone can be used to crush someone else's skull, using far more lethal firearms calls for a certain amount of knowledge and experience. A culture of firearms is not uniformly distributed among the population: for instance, it is much more common among men than women. This gender difference helps explain why voluntary killings by women are considerably rarer than those by men.

Second, culture provides ways of organizing experiences and classifying the various types of situation we find ourselves in, so that we can make what we believe to be an appropriate response. Consequently, culture affects whether a social actor will define a certain situation as one in which violence, or even killing, is demanded. We will return to the question of defining a situation as an occasion for homicide in the section on the interactionist approach.

According to the culturalist perspective, all societies comprise diverse social groups with very different conceptions of good and evil, of lawful and unlawful, and of right and wrong, which are transmitted to the group's new members via a process of socialization (Brookman, 2005). Thus, each society will have certain cultural models that reject the dominant middle class values regarding, for example, the family, work, the acceptable means of improving one's status and the legitimacy of acts of violence. Such models are embraced by groups that often belong to the deprived classes: in the case of the United States, young black men.

For the culturalist perspective on homicide, two theoretical frameworks are of particular importance: subcultural theories, and differential association theory. These approaches will be discussed in the following pages.

Subcultural Theories

Subcultural theories encompass approaches that differ in far from negligible ways, making it impossible to refer to a single theory. Here, we will deal with the three best-known approaches, which have had the greatest impact on subsequent theoretical and empirical research: Cohen's delinquent subculture theory (1955), Cloward and Ohlin's differential opportunity theory (1960), and Wolfgang and Ferracuti's subculture of violence theory (1967). Intellectually, these theories are part of the tradition stemming from the Chicago School and Merton's notion of anomie (Williams & McShane, 1994). The different approaches based on the idea of subculture fall under the absence or deficit paradigm mentioned earlier (Prina, 2019).

Cohen's delinquent subculture theory (1955) starts from the observation that criminal behavior is most frequent among gangs of young working class males. According to Cohen – who refers explicitly to Merton's strain theory – all individuals seek social status, but do not have equal opportunities for reaching it. The sons of families belonging to the deprived classes are at a major disadvantage compared to their middle class counterparts, which causes a status frustration that can lead to a collective adaptation. This adaptation serves to construct new norms and new criteria for defining status that legitimize the characteristics of lower class individuals and the types of behavior they are able to enact. A new cultural model is thus created, a delinquent subculture characterized by behavior that is malicious, negativistic and non-utilitarian – where there is no rationale for delinquency other than seeking peer status (Williams & McShane, 1994). This subculture accepts lethal violence and sees it as legitimate in some situations. Consequently, it is the need for status that generates the delinquent subculture, which is a solution available to individuals who have no other way of achieving success. The more a person from a deprived background interacts with a delinquent subculture, the more likely he is to adopt its values and behavior to satisfy his need for status.

Cloward and Ohlin's theory (1960) also draws on strain theory to understand criminal behavior. These scholars agree with Merton on the importance of reaching socially prescribed goals. However, they depart from Merton in noting that there is not one, but two opportunity structures whereby individuals can achieve their aims: the legitimate structure and the equally important illegitimate structure. Lower class youths – unlike those from the middle and upper classes – have few opportunities for achieving prescribed statuses via the legitimate structure, and can thus decide to turn to the illegitimate one.

Not all individuals, however, take the same route through the illegitimate structure: different delinquent subcultures can develop, depending on the characteristics of the urban area concerned, the level of integration between the various individuals who are drawn into criminal circles, and between the legitimate and illegitimate structures. The so-called criminal subculture will arise in neighborhoods that are not excessively degraded and have a certain degree of integration between crime and conventional institutions. Its primary goal is to make money though illicit means with relatively low levels of violence, providing a set of services to conventional society – gambling, drugs and prostitution. The most frequent crimes are thus theft, robbery, extortion, drug dealing, receiving stolen goods and exploitation of prostitution. Gangs are stratified hierarchically by age, with adults directing the younger members' illicit activities. Clearly, in a subculture of this kind, lethal violence is a last resort, as it is at odds with the delinquents' goals.

The conflict subculture, on the other hand, develops in the more disorganized neighborhoods, where there is no well-organized illegal structure to exercise strong social control over young delinquents. In this case, individuals employ violence as a means of gaining respect, honor and dignity, and to control their territory, which they see as part of their identity; gangs thus show violent, uncontrolled and unpredictable behavior. They are unstable groups, consisting of people who are failures in crime by comparison with the organized groups typical of the criminal subculture, who are well integrated with each other and with conventional society (Williams & McShane, 1994). In the conflict subculture, violence is decidedly more frequent, as it serves to reach the goals outlined above in certain situations.

Independently of whether the criminal or conflict subculture predominates in a given area, there are individuals who are unable to access either the legitimate or the illegitimate opportunity structure. These actors have thus failed in two ways, and develop what is called the retreatist subculture. This subculture is primarily oriented towards drug consumption, and criminal behavior serves to obtain the money to buy drugs. In the retreatist subculture, lethal violence is rarer than in the conflict subculture, as it is not a means of achieving status, but arises out of an extreme need for money or the total confusion occasioned by substance abuse.

Wolfgang and Ferracuti's subculture of violence theory is the approach that centers most on understanding homicide (Brookman, 2005), as it draws specifically on Wolfgang's first studies of lethal violence (1958). According to Wolfgang and Ferracuti, not all subcultures that reject the values of mainstream society embrace others that are entirely opposed or in sharp contrast with them. Attention should thus focus on people belonging to the so-called subculture of violence, whose members share a favorable attitude to violent and brutal acts, and are socialized to engage in them. People who commit violence and homicide without belonging to the subculture of violence exhibit clear personality disorders and greater sense of guilt and anxiety than perpetrators who are part of this subculture (Williams & McShane, 1994).

From this theory's standpoint, homicide chiefly occurs among the deprived social classes, and in many cases arises from incidents that are relatively trivial in origin, such as minor insults or scuffles. The subculture of violence, in fact, encourages the use of force – even if it turns fatal – in the name of an exaggerated sense of values such as honor, courage and manliness, and individual characteristics such as physical prowess. Accordingly, high homicide rates are due to a cultural environment of shared values and norms that are favorable to, and can even encourage, a practice that mainstream culture considers extremely deviant (Brookman, 2005).

Anderson (1994, cited in Corzine et al., 1999) speaks of a true "code of the streets", that includes an extremely low tolerance for personal affronts by others and a strong emphasis on the ideals of respect and honor, which must be defended at all costs, including one's life. Given the ambiguous nature of many social interactions, adherents of this code can erupt in violence even when there is no good reason, as in the case where one social actor interprets another's eye contact as a challenge of some kind. Even a person who has nothing to do with the code of the streets can end up being involved in this sort of situation, being unable to avoid dealing with an adherent of the code, in the wrong place and at the wrong time.

Differential Association Theory

The first version of this theory was advanced in 1939 by Edwin Sutherland in the third edition of his *Principles of Criminology*, while the final version was presented in the last, 1947, edition of the book. Sutherland – whose thinking was further elucidated by other scholars (Cressey, 1964; Matza, 1969) – is one of the founders of so-called sociological criminology, as he forged an alliance between the disciplines of criminology and sociology (Williams & McShane, 1994). Differential association theory fits into the broader presence or conditioning paradigm that underscores the importance of learning in deviant and criminal behavior (Prina, 2019).

One of the core concepts in Sutherland's proposed framework is that of differential social organization: in highly differentiated modern society, there is a multitude of groups – called associations – in which individuals interact in more or less stable ways. As members of these associations, individuals learn a plurality of behaviors that are in line with or opposed to the lawful norms of conventional society. The term differential association is used because the content transmitted by the associations varies according to the people in them, and can differ in the importance assigned to obeying the law. Consequently, individuals' proclivity for crime, and for homicidal violence, will also depend on the value constellation held by their associates, and in particular by those associates they regard as most important and with whom they have interacted most frequently over a long period. Nevertheless, the choice of behavior does not depend only on the influence to which social actors are exposed, but also on the lack of alternative role models, criminal or otherwise (Williams & McShane, 1994).

In Sutherland's view, crime is the consequence of a culture conflict: an individual commits crimes because this choice is consistent with the values of the association he belongs to, which, however, are not in line with those of conventional society. Social differentiation increases the culture conflict, given that it produces a set of values and interests that differ among various social groups, some of which are covered by legal safeguards. Groups with divergent values and lifestyles come into conflict with the dominant authority, resulting in higher crime rates.

Another key concept in differential association theory is that of learning: criminal behaviors are learned through association in intimate personal groups, in a process of normal interactive communication (Williams & McShane, 1994). Not surprisingly, this approach provided the foundation for the later theories proposed by several interactionist scholars (see, for example, H. S. Becker, 1963; Lemert, 1967) who focus their attention on deviant experience as a gradual process of learning motivations, rules and techniques, as well as of acquiring a criminal identity (Prina, 2019).

According to Sutherland, there are two main components of learning. First, the techniques of crime, which indicate *how* to be a criminal: how to pick a pocket without being detected, how to crack a safe, how to use a firearm to threaten, and if necessary kill. These skills can be quite complex. The other content of learning consists of the definitions that justify and support criminal behavior – the values, motivations, attitudes and rationalizations – or in other words, *why* to be a criminal: why it is right to rob someone, why someone deserves to be killed, and so forth.

Sutherland assigns greater importance to learning the definitions of criminal behaviors than to learning the techniques: a person turns to crime when the definitions favorable to breaking the law exceed those that are favorable to conventional behavior, not just in a numerical sense, but also in terms of the quality and intimacy of the relationship with the members of the association. As regards technique, most criminal behaviors require no more than can be learned in the arena of conventional behavior. This is to some extent true in the case of lethal violence: while it takes a certain amount of technical competence to kill someone with a firearm, other ways of killing (stabbing, strangling or using blunt instruments, for example) do not call for any specific expertise.

It should also be emphasized that the processes of learning to be a criminal are not substantially different from those involved in learning conventional social norms: the fundamental difference lies in what is learned, not in how it is learned. Moreover, everyone can learn deviant and criminal behaviors, whatever their economic and social condition; Sutherland's approach thus has the merit of contemplating more than the poor and deprived population that was the primary focus of the theories we have discussed so far. Not coincidentally, this scholar is also known for his pioneering work on white collar crime (Sutherland, 1949).

THE INTERACTIONIST PERSPECTIVE

The structuralist and culturalist approaches to homicidal violence share one important shortcoming: they tell us nothing about the micro-level level dynamics that actually lead individuals – whether for structural reasons or for cultural reasons – to commit a crime as serious as homicide. Strain theory, for instance, cannot explain why the vast majority of people in a condition of relative deprivation do *not* kill or commit other acts of violence (Brookman, 2005). Observing homicide from the standpoint of gender provides further confirmation: why do women kill much less than men, even though their position in the social strata is lower on average? Similarly, not everyone who comes into contact with a violent subculture finds themselves caught up in episodes of physical aggression, and only very few such episodes end in homicide. Essentially, the structuralist and culturalist approaches risk being overly deterministic: these theoretical frameworks are necessary in order to pinpoint the social and cultural settings where episodes of lethal violence are more likely to occur, but they cannot explain why a certain person in such a setting will kill and another will not.

Starting in the 1960s, a theoretical corpus began to take shape in criminality studies (H. S. Becker, 1963; H. S. Becker, 1974; Erikson, 1966; Goffman, 1963b; Kitsuse & Cicourel, 1963; Lemert, 1967; Matza, 1969; Sykes & Matza, 1957) which built on the more general approach taken by symbolic interactionism (Blumer, 1969; Cooley, 1902; Mead, 1934). The interactionist perspective takes issue with both the excessive determinism of the approaches that had been used to date, and the attempt to understand criminal behavior entirely in terms of the role played by macro-level (or, at most, meso-level) variables. To overcome these limitations, attention focuses on the so-called situational elements (see, for example, Miethe & Regoeczi 2004): criminal acts, including homicides, are committed during face-to-face interactions between social actors. To fully understand these acts, it is thus necessary to focus on a series of relational and interpretive micro-dynamics. This approach draws on the presence or conditioning paradigm mentioned above (Prina, 2019).

What, then, is the explanatory contribution that the interactionist perspective makes to understanding a phenomenon as complex, heterogeneous and multidimensional as homicide? First of all, it changes the level of analysis from the macro to the micro. The importance of the context is not called into question, but analysis centers on the micro-context where the killing takes place. In addition, attention focuses, not on the homicide rate, but on another equally important aspect of the phenomenon: why did the interaction between *those* two social actors result in bloodshed, rather than having a less dramatic ending?

The interactionist perspective is not especially good at casting light on instrumental homicides: in particular, on impersonal killings such as those in the world of organized crime, which involve people who are unknown to each other. Even here, however, this perspective still has a contribution to make: it helps provide an understanding of the interactional dynamics that lead a social actor to become a hit man for the mob.

By contrast, the interactionist approach is particularly useful for understanding expressive homicides, both when the actors involved already knew each other, and in the case of altercations between strangers that spiral out of control, since it retraces the interactional chain that led to the death of one of the two contenders.

Though the interactionist perspective was developed later than the structuralist and culturalist approaches, its foundations were laid long before it was formalized. As indicated above, the Chicago School had noted the importance of self-construction through interactions with others in the development of deviant careers, while Sutherland's differential association theory had also emphasized that interaction with members of significant associations is fundamental in learning criminal behavior.

One of the first major contributions of the interactional perspective was to emphasize that individuals' responses to specific situations are flexible rather than rigorously deterministic, and that there is a plurality of social values and behaviors rather than a general consensus about what is right and wrong (Brookman, 2005). For example, Matza (1964, cited in Brookman, 2005) claims that gang members are only partially committed to a subculture opposing conventional society, and drift in and out of deviant activity because society does not have a set of basic core values. What is found in reality, in fact, is a plurality in which deviant and non-deviant individuals continually overlap and interact. This line of thinking led to what came to be known as labeling theory (see, for example, H. S. Becker, 1963; H. S. Becker, 1974), where attention focuses on the definitions whereby individuals and society identify which types of behavior are deviant and which are not, what forms of reaction and control should follow deviant behavior, and the repercussions that labeling individuals as deviant have on their identity and thus on creating and reinforcing deviance (Prina, 2019). Though undeniably important, this approach to deviance and criminality will not be discussed in detail here for reasons of parsimony, as labeling theories concentrate primarily on so-called victimless crimes (e.g., drug dealing and use, prostitution, etc.), rather than those involving brutal violence. In the following pages, we will deal with another strand of interactional thinking that focuses more specifically on understanding homicide. Before leaving labeling theory, however, it should be pointed out that its notion of career deviance can be of some use in explaining homicide. Deviant behavior is also due to conventional society's reaction to deviance, as in the case, for example, of learning to be violent in prison. The notion of career deviance provides a sequential model of interpreting deviance on the basis of the interaction between conventional society and the actors diverging from it: there is a progressive acquisition of a deviant identity, a slow assimilation of the motivations that justify deviance, and a process of learning the techniques needed to put deviant behavior into practice (Prina, 2019). In many cases, then, homicide can be regarded as the culmination – given its seriousness – of a deviant career that the actor has embarked on gradually.

In addition to analyze labeling's effects on creating deviance, interactionist scholars have addressed the interactions between criminals and their victims. Testifying to their importance, these interactions are one of the prime concerns of victimology (see, in this connection, the pioneering work ofVon Hentig, 1948), the branch of criminology that studies the victims of crime and everything connected to them. Criminal-victim interactions make a crucial contribution to generating – or not generating – the conditions that spark an episode of lethal violence (Brookman, 2005): obvious though it might seem, we must not forget that a homicide would not be possible if offender and victim were not in the same place at the same time, linked by an interaction that may be minimal – for example, a bystander who witnesses a bank robbery and is killed as a result – or intimate and prolonged – as in the case of a woman who mortally wounds her spouse after putting up with violence and abuse for years.

An important concept in the interactional dynamics between the parties involved in an episode of lethal violence is victim-precipitation, which Wolfgang introduced in his 1958 book on homicide. According to Wolfgang, this is a situation where the victim is the first in the homicide drama to use physical force directed at his subsequent slayer[*]. Thus, in homicides precipitated by the victim, which party is killed and which deals the fatal blow may be a matter of chance. Consequently, concentrating only on the characteristics of offenders and the dynamics affecting them, as the theories we have examined so far have done, stands very much in the way of achieving a real understanding of the reasons underlying an episode of lethal violence.

---

[*] As regards its benefit in understanding crime generally, the notion of victim-precipitation has attracted much criticism, not all of which is unjustified (Brookman, 2005). However, it is an important analytical tool for the interactionist approach to homicide, as it provides an interesting lens for observing the interaction between perpetrators of lethal violence and their victims.

Over the decades, interactionist studies of homicide have gone well beyond simply extending attention to the victim. The concept of victim-precipitation is thus only a starting point: trying simply to understand who lit the fuse of violence, in fact, tells us relatively little about the processual nature of a homicide and the set of interactional dynamics linking the offender, the victim and any bystanders. Later theoretical work by Luckenbill (1977) made a major step forward in this connection, as it specifically sought to understand the dynamics that lead to homicide, rather than to deviance or criminality in general. Before turning our attention to this approach, however, a few words are in order concerning the micro-context surrounding the interactions between the protagonists of a homicide.

Analyzing a number of empirical studies, Brookman (2005) notes that lethal episodes are not randomly distributed through space and time. There are a series of elements, called situational factors, that create a micro-environment where recourse to fatal violence is more frequent (in this connection, see also Luckenbill, 1977). This type of episode occurs more frequently in certain locations than in others: in pubs, discos and night spots in general, as well as in their immediate surroundings (parking lots, alleys). Many homicides take place during the night and at weekends, when these venues are most crowded. Other situational factors, which not coincidentally are linked to these places and times, include alcohol and drug consumption, which can make disputes and altercations more likely to end in violence.

Moreover, Luckenbill (1977) found that most occasions of homicide were loose, informal affairs in leisure settings: an evening at home watching the television, a get-together with friends at a tavern, cruising about town, and so on. In such settings, a plurality of behaviors – not always countenanced by prevailing social norms – can be adopted without necessarily having to fear much censure by one's social group: drinking or taking drugs, an unsolicited compliment to an unknown woman, a rude remark to someone outside the group, over-insistently eyeing someone else's girlfriend, etc. As we have seen, however, such behavior can set off a spiral of violence, or contribute to it getting out of hand.

Lethal violence is rarer in work settings, or in tighter occasions of leisure such as baptisms, weddings and funerals. As these situations are bound by strict social expectations regarding the roles of the interacting actors and their behavior, there is less room for the kind of actions listed above. Luckenbill (1977) also emphasizes that in occasions of homicide, the interaction is most frequently between people who are closely related by marriage, kinship or friendship. Even where offender and victim do not have such a relationship, one or both are often in the company of their intimates.

One example of the kind of micro-environment favorable to homicide that we have just described would be the parking lot of a night spot during the weekend, where an altercation breaks out in the early hours of the morning between two groups of men who have been drinking or taking drugs. If the interactional dynamics described in the following section develop in such a situation, an altercation of relatively trivial origin can degenerate into homicide.

Homicide as a Situated Transaction

This approach was proposed by David Luckenbill (1977), building on the theoretical foundations laid down in the writings of Erving Goffmann (1963a, 1967, 1969). Luckenbill formulated his theses by scrutinizing 70 cases of criminal homicide occurring over a ten-year period in California.

Luckenbill sees homicide as the fatal outcome of an intense and conflictual interchange between the offender, the victim and any bystanders. The interactional dynamics culminating in murder involve the joint contribution of the soon-to-be offender and the soon-to-be victim to a "character contest" in which each contender seeks to save face – in other words, social value and dignity, or the self-image to be maintained in the course of a critical interaction – at the other's expense. To do so, the contenders stand steady in the face of adversity, regardless of the consequences this entails. For these dynamics to result in lethal violence, there must be a consensus among participants that the use of force is a suitable if not required means of settling the contest.

Luckenbill refers to this chain of interaction between two or more individuals that lasts the time they find themselves together in one place as a "situated transaction". Often, however, homicide does not result from a single chain of interaction: in many cases, the episode of lethal violence is preceded by other chains of interaction between offender and victim, in a crescendo of hostilities and, sometimes, physical violence that could be termed rehearsals.

According to Luckenbill, the situated transactions that culminate in a homicide resemble what Lyman and Scott (1970), taking their cue from Goffmann (1967), call "face games": the offender and the victim make "moves" in this game on the basis of the other's moves and the position of their audience of bystanders, if any. It is this interplay of moves that produces the event's fatal outcome.

Naturally, the contenders' moves in a face game ending in murder vary from case to case. However, we can identify six time-ordered stages common to all. Before going into the details of each stage, it should be pointed out that Lukenbill's approach emphasizes the processual character of the murderous episode, where the statuses of offender and victim are not necessarily determined beforehand: in many cases, the person who in the early stages of the transaction was cast as the offender ends up being killed by the person initially cast as his victim. In the first five stages described below, the label of offender will be assigned to the contender who first states his intention to kill or injure the other, considered as the potential victim. In the sixth stage, on the other hand, the label of offender is assigned to the individual who in fact dealt the fatal blow, and the victim is the person who had the worst of the battle.

In the first stage of the transaction, the victim makes an opening move that the offender could perceive as an offense to "face", or self-image. This is a pivotal event in the relationship between the contenders, as it disrupts the social order that until that moment characterized the interaction between the two. This initiates a process that will transform the previous, unstrained, exchange into a transaction involving conflict and the use of violence. The form and content of the victim's first move depend on circumstances, but we can distinguish between three different types: a verbal expression that the offender interprets as offensive, refusal to cooperate or comply with one or more requests by the offender – who thus sees his authority called into question – and lastly, a physical or otherwise nonverbal gesture that the offender finds personally offensive (for instance, a betrayal, which calls his sexual prowess into question).

In the second stage, the offender interprets the victim's first move as personally offensive. In some instances, the victim may have been unwittingly offensive, as in the case of a small child who cries from hunger, and continues to do so even when his father tells him to stop, since he is too young to understand the order. Not knowing this, the father could interpret the persistent crying as a challenge to his authority. In many cases, however, the victim does in fact intend to be offensive. Even If the victim's desire to offend is not immediately clear, it can be perceived by the offender on the basis of previous experience of similar events where the victim's intentions were obvious, or the offender may learn of it from inquiries made of the victim or audience.

In the third stage, the offender must deal with the real or presumed affront. Here, the offender is up against a dilemma: should he avoid escalation, accepting the loss of face, or react with an equally hostile move, standing his ground and thus saving his social value and dignity? It goes without saying that in the transactions that end in a homicide, the second option is chosen. The offender thus expresses anger and contempt for the victim, generally issuing a verbal or physical, but nonlethal, challenge to the victim, though in some cases, the victim is killed in this stage. In the case of a nonlethal interaction, the most frequent reaction is an ultimatum: the victim is told to take back the offending statement or stop the hostile action, or face physical harm or even death. Essentially, the offender makes his first move to save face at this stage. Through a hostile reaction, the offender implicitly suggests to the victim that the situation is one in which violence and aggression are suitable and necessary for settling the question.

In the fourth stage, the victim is placed in the same dilemma the offender was in earlier: should he continue with the hostile interaction, demonstrating strength of character, or flee the situation and restore social order, withdrawing all challenges to the offender's face but putting one's own in jeopardy? Generally, the victim refuses to demonstrate weakness and thus doubles down, implicitly agreeing with the offender that violence is a suitable means of resolving the dispute. The victim's most common reaction is to ignore the offender's threats and continue the offensive action. There are cases where the victim does not decide to escalate the situation intentionally, but this is not understood by the offender. This is what happens in our earlier example of the crying child: the father interprets the crying as a challenge to his authority, even though the child is far from having such an intention. A second possible response is physical aggression, while in other cases the victim issues a counter-challenge in the form of an ultimatum or by calling the offender's bluff. In this stage, any bystanders also play a role: they may encourage one contender or the other, cheering them toward violence, or remain neutral. Inaction, however, can be interpreted by the offender or the victim as implicit support for escalating hostilities.

In the fifth stage, both contenders have a working agreement that the situation is one where violence is appropriate. Both the offender and the victim, then, have contributed to the development of a potentially fatal transaction. The confrontation is further aggravated if weapons are available, reinforcing the credibility of the threats and challenges. In this stage, it is the offender who has a weapon capable of overcoming the victim. In some cases, the weapon is already on the scene, either because the offender is usually armed, or – more rarely – because the offender brought it on the assumption that it would be needed, as a problem was expected. In most cases, however, the offender leaves the scene temporarily to secure a firearm or knife, or uses an everyday object found at hand – a pillow, telephone cord, a heavy ornament – as a lethal weapon. Possessing weapons makes battle possible, and likely in situations where violence is considered necessary. The dynamics of the fatal battle can vary widely. In many cases, the episode is brief and precise: at times, a single shot, stab or rally of blows is all the offender needs to kill the victim; at other times there is an exchange in which the offender prevails.

In the sixth and last stage, the victim is dead and the transaction terminates in one of three possible moves: the offender flees in most cases, but in others will voluntarily remain on the scene until the police arrive. More rarely, bystanders will hold the offender for the police. Which alternative is chosen depends on two distinct lines of influence: the relationship between the offender and the victim, and the audience's position regarding the offense. When there is no audience and the offender and victim were intimately related, the offender remains on the scene and notifies the police – sometimes quickly, sometimes less so. In the meantime, the offender checks the victim's condition, and thinks about what happened and its consequences. By contrast, when there was little or no relationship between the contenders, the offender typically flees the scene. If there is an audience, it now replaces the victim as the primary interactant, and its attitude will influence the offender's moves. If the bystanders are hostile, they generally convince the offender to remain on the scene and surrender to the police. If they are neutral, the offender escapes, taking advantage of their shock. If the bystanders are supportive of the offender, they assist his escape and deny his responsibility when first questioned by the police.

Violentization Theory

Violentization theory was proposed by Lonnie Athens (1980, 1989; see also Rhodes, 2000). Of the various interactionist views of deviant behavior, this approach – like that regarding situated transactions between offender and victim – is particularly relevant to the study of homicide, and will thus be discussed in some depth here.

Athens's attention is not focused on deviance and criminality in general, or on violence per se or the individuals who under certain circumstances could be violent. Rather, he is concerned with dangerous criminals who have already committed particularly brutal acts of violence such as murder. Athens's chief interest lies in crimes where provocation and aggression are abnormally disproportionate. While Luckenbill's theory emphasizes the chain of interaction between offender, victim and any witnesses to lethal violence, Athens concentrates on the offender, analyzing his past and present interactions in his context and how they have been interpreted. It is precisely these interpretations, in fact, that lead the individual to develop a marked tendency towards particularly brutal forms of violence.

Athens's theoretical framework builds on the thinking of Herbert Blumer (1969), one of the fathers of symbolic interactionism. Blumer maintained that social reality is a vast interpretive process in which people, singly and collectively, guide themselves by defining objects, events and situations which they encounter. Social action – whatever form it takes – must be investigated from the standpoint of the actor engaged in it: in this way, we will be able to understand the elements taken into consideration, how they are interpreted, the array of counter-actions that could be taken in that situation and the actor's interpretations that result in one such action being chosen. What is needed, then, is an analysis of the action's career (Rhodes, 2000). In Blumer's view, if we focus on acts of extreme violence that can end in homicide, we must seek to understand how the actor dealt with his tendency to take actions that are so strongly opposed by conventional society; this, in fact, is what is entailed by Mead's concepts of "I" and "Me" (Rhodes, 2000).

Athens's theory sets out to answer the question: how does a violent nature arise and develop in some individuals, and ends by guiding their actions? In other words: how does one become a dangerous violent criminal? Answering this question, Athens maintains, calls for a new theory that integrates social environmental and bio-physiological factors[*]. The bridging concept that can integrate these factors is that of social experience, which emerges from the interaction between a social actor, his environment, and the interpretive and personal choices the actor makes in specific situations. Some social experiences are so significant,

---

[*] In reality, according to Bean (1990), Athens draws extensively on earlier approaches such as the labeling, subculture and differential association theories.

consequential and unforgettable that they act as catalysts, leading individuals to resort to extreme violence in situations where there is little or no provocation by the other party.

It should be emphasized that the social experiences that turn people into violent criminals do not occur all at once, but take place gradually over time. Such experiences, moreover, often build on earlier social experiences. It is thus reasonable to assume that there is a developmental process with discernable stages. This is a social process, based on interaction with others.

Athens thus sought to identify the chain of traumatic social experiences that were decisive in the formation of violent criminals. To do so, he conducted in-depth interviews with 38 criminals imprisoned for particularly heinous acts of violence and two "quasi-control groups", one consisting of nonviolent criminals, and the other of six women who had been victims of domestic assault.

What Athens calls the violentization process consists of four distinct stages: brutalization, belligerency, violent performances and virulency. Each stage is characterized by different social experiences. Completing one stage depends on having undergone all of the experiences characterizing it (though not necessarily always in the same order), and completing the entire process requires that all four stages be passed through in sequence. It should be pointed out that the first stages of the process make the subsequent stages possible but not inevitable. The first stages may be completed without entering the next ones, and it may be that many more people start upon the process than finish it. Completing the whole process takes a number of years, though in a rare cases a few months may be sufficient. For males, the process typically begins in prepubescence and ends in the mid- to late teens; for females, on the other hand, the process is completed later. At the end of the process, the social actor has gone full circle, inflicting on others the suffering and pain he or she suffered in the past.

The first stage, brutalization, takes place in one of the individual's primary groups, i.e., those characterized by intimate face-to-face association. This stage often occurs in the family setting, but other groups may be involved, for example in a gang or in prison, between teenage or adult convicts. Brutalization comprises a trilogy of elemental experiences: violent subjugation, personal horrification and violent coaching. In violent subjugation, the victim of the process (referred to hereunder as the "subject") undergoes acts of violence by an authority figure, usually a parent. The purpose of these acts is to compel the subject's complete submission, and the unconditional acknowledgement of the perpetrator's power. Subjugation may be coercive or retaliatory. In the first case, the authority figure threatens or uses violence to persuade a defiant subject to obey; in the second case, the use of force is a punishment for some past or present disobedience on the part of the subject. For the latter, retaliatory subjugation has more traumatic consequences, as violence continues well beyond the point where the subject signals submission and does not end with a pledge of obedience, as in the case of coercive subjugation.

In personal horrification, the subject does not himself experience violent subjugation, but witnesses – sees or in some cases only hears – another member of his primary group with whom he has a special relationship undergoing it: his mother, sister, a very close friend. Compared to violent subjugation, personal horrification is less traumatic for the subject at the physical level, but not from the psychological standpoint: this social experience, in fact, produce feelings of impotence and a deep sense of guilt that linger long after the immediate experience, along with rage and contempt for the aggressor.

Violent coaching consists of prompting the subject to use violence, but in a way that is informal and implicit. The violent coach is a member of the primary group, usually older than the subject: the father, older brother, uncle or an older friend; in some cases, there may be more than one coach. Given their greater experience, coaches believe they have the right or obligation to instruct the subject about how to deal with conflictive situations. The aim of violent coaching is not to teach how to inflict physical harm at the practical level, but to transmit the idea that severely wounding a contender is a personal responsibility they cannot evade, but must discharge regardless of whether they are a man or a woman, young or old. The subject is thus instructed to be forceful, dominant and self-reliant in any dispute.

The belligerency stage is a brooding period, in which the subject realizes that a strategy is needed in order to avoid further episodes of brutalization in the future. For the first time, the subject also grasps the scope, value and content of the coaching he has received. At the end of this stage, there is a first, mitigated resolution to use violence. The subject realizes that it is a useful tool in certain specific situations: when severely provoked, or when he understands that he would be able to prevail. In this stage, however, the use of violence remains on an abstract plane, as it is not reflected in the subject's actual conduct.

In the third stage, that of violent performances, the subject is in a condition to translate the resolutions made in the previous stage into concrete action. This is a complex and delicate passage, given that attacking someone with a brutality that can lead to death places the subject's physical safety, freedom and psychological wellbeing at considerable risk. As mentioned earlier, the subject is initially willing to use violence only in certain circumscribed situations. One of the factors that influence this stage is the outcome of the first violent altercation, which can end in a victory if the subject inflicts grievous injuries on the antagonist, in a defeat in the opposite case, or in a draw if the battle is interrupted when the contenders have done serious harm to each other. Draws leave the subject in a state of limbo in the present stage, while victories encourage more and more violence. Defeats, on the other hand, can lead the subject to desist, concluding that he has little aptitude for violence. In some situations, however, a defeat can make the subject even more dangerous, persuading him that he should resort to more effective and lethal forms of violence in future altercations.

The fourth stage, virulency, marks the passage from a mitigated use of violence as described in the previous stage to an unmitigated one. A series of victories in physical altercations will not be enough to persuade the subject to become a ruthless aggressor. For this to happen, the subject must gain violent notoriety: his victories must receive social recognition from his primary and secondary groups, as well as from members of institutions such as school officials, the police, prosecutors and judges. This is perhaps the point of greatest contact between Athens's thinking and labeling theory: to become a more violent person, the subject must be labeled as such. His violent notoriety makes the subject feared and in some cases respected, generating in others what Athens calls social trepidation – the same trepidation that the subject felt towards his tormentor in the brutalization stage. This trepidation produces a number of major changes in the subject's sense of identity. In the light of others' fear of him, the subject is freed of his own fear of being brutalized or beaten again; consequently, he feels he can interact with others in whatever way he wants, without being afraid to provoke them or challenge them openly. The subject takes pride in his violent actions and develops a sense of omnipotence and invincibility, leading him to make a far more extreme use of violence than before: feeling that he benefits from his violent acts, the subject is now willing to attack, harm and kill with minimal or no provocation. Paradoxically, the subject has become a ruthless aggressor exactly like the hated and despised brutalizer who victimized him in the past.

CONCLUSION

The structuralist, culturalist and interactionist perspectives are often considered as alternatives, while some of the scholars who adopt one of them not infrequently stress that their own choice is incompatible with the other theoretical frameworks. In reality, as we have seen, a full understanding of a phenomenon as multidimensional, complex and heterogeneous as homicide can be gained only by triangulating these three perspectives. Even in order to understand deviant and criminal behavior in general, in any case, there is a call to develop an integrated perspective, building on the foundations laid down by a number of different theories. This makes it possible to observe the interwoven influence of different planes – from the general to the particular, and vice versa – while also considering the role of individual social actors' choices and personal traits

(Prina, 2019). In connection with personal traits, mention should be made of the recent genetic and neuroscience research on criminal behavior. Apart from the studies that fall into naïve determinism and oversimplification, there is now a broad consensus that genetic factors and neurological components have a role to play, though exactly where this role begins and ends is not yet clear. Undoubtedly, these elements do not determine specific behaviors mechanistically, though they may influence a given character trait or a particular form of conduct. In addition, they interact with and are influenced by the characteristics of the actor's social, cultural and relational context, with the opportunities and constraints that it offers (Prina, 2019).

The structuralist and culturalist approaches have long been thought of as being in opposition to each other. Structure is a concrete fact, located outside the individual Self, whereas culture is collective, but subjective, inside the mind of the individual (Alexander & Thompson, 2008). In reality, the two approaches have more points in common than differences; rather than alternatives, it would be more correct to say that they are complementary. To begin with, they share the same macro-level outlook. Both, in fact, explain the different homicide rates among groups with different social characteristics. The fact that some of these differences are structural and some are cultural is not all that important: it goes without saying that both of these dimensions have a crucial role in reconstructing the context in which episodes of lethal violence occur most frequently. Corzine and colleagues (1999) have advanced an interesting hypothesis in this connection: they argue that structural conditions such as poverty and social inequality lead to the development of a constellation of values that encourages and facilitates violence, including lethal violence. In this case, then, culture is an intervening factor that helps explain the dynamics whereby structural conditions influence homicide rates.

In any case, that structure and culture both contribute to explaining homicide is clear when we go into the details of their respective theories and see their similarities and cross-references. Many of the arguments offered by structuralist theories hinge on certain eminently cultural dynamics which are simply taken to be implicit. The very concept of institution, one of the pillars of the social structure, ties in with the cultural dimension of society, as it is not only a relatively stable configuration of situations and roles, but also of values and norms. In addition, two important theories employing the concept of subculture – Cohen's (1955) and Cloward and Ohlin's (1960) – build explicitly on strain theory, adding the cultural dimension as the means of reducing anomie. Even Merton's strain theory – a quintessentially structuralist formulation – would not hold water were it not for the fundamental role it assigns to culture. Strain, in fact, is set up across two poles: the cultural structure of a society – its values, which prescribe goals to be reached via certain means it sees as legitimate – and its social structure, or in other words, the unequal distribution of opportunities for success among the actors.

Social disorganization theory, moreover, emphasizes that the loss of shared values plays a major role in the weakening of primary social relationships that takes place in large cities. This leads to a lack of clear norms guiding individuals' behavior. In addition, this theory stresses that one of the reasons for the erosion of social control in a community is the lack of shared values resulting from population turnover and migratory flows.

Lastly, social control theory also entails references to cultural elements, though less markedly than in the examples we have just given. What, for instance, is responsible for the weakening of social structure and institutions, which jeopardizes their ability to curb social actors' selfish interests? The thought that springs to mind is that behind such a significant change, there must have been major transformations in values and norms.

The structuralist and culturalist perspectives, in addition to sharing many features, also have a major risk in common: their excessive determinism, since they pay little attention to the individual level micro-dynamics that explain why some people in a given structural and/or cultural context will kill and others will not. To fully understand homicide, the theoretical work stemming from the interactionist perspective is thus of considerable importance, as it focuses specifically on these dynamics. Undoubtedly, the interactionist perspective is farther from the structuralist and culturalist approaches than the latter are from each other. Nevertheless, considering the interactionist theories to be incompatible alternatives to the others would be reductive. Again, we can say that they are complementary: rather than disproving structuralist and culturalist thinking, interactionism shines light on areas that these approaches do not contemplate.

The interactionist perspective also has several points in common with the culturalist and structuralist approaches, the former in particular. One of the characteristics of subcultures discussed by culturalist theoreticians is the exaggerated sense of honor, respect and courage, as values to be defended at all costs, including that of taking another human being's life. When Luckenbill refers to the social actor who is willing to use physical violence to defend and save face – in other words, his social value and dignity – he is expressing a substantially similar concept. Not coincidentally, both the culturalist and the interactionist approach emphasize that the motives for homicide are often relatively trivial: eyeing someone's girlfriend too insistently, for example, or a risqué comment. According to violentization theory, moreover, one of the social experiences that takes place in the brutalization stage consists of coaching in the use of violence by one or more members of the primary group, usually older than the subject. Here, it is hard not to see a clear reflection of Sutherland's differential association theory, where learning criminal behavior by association in intimate personal groups is crucial. Lastly, culture is fundamental in whether a social actor defines a given situation as one that calls for physical violence; as we know, the concept of defining the situation is also of major importance from the interactionist standpoint.

However, even though interactionist theorists criticize the structuralists' and culturalists' excessive determinism, their own formulations are by no means immune from this risk. According to Bean (1990), violentization theory also takes an excessively universal and deterministic view: all actors who complete the four stages described by Athens are fated to become dangerous violent criminals, regardless of their age, social class, ethnicity, educational level and so forth, providing that their attitudes and physical abilities enable them to commit violent acts. Luckenbill's chain of interactions at the basis of an episode of lethal violence could also be accused of over-determinism, if the passage from one stage to another is interpreted as taking place mechanistically and inescapably, independently of the characteristics of the individuals involved.

Another limitation of the interactionist approach is that it focuses only on the micro-interactions between actors, neglecting the dynamics involving the more general context and society as a whole. As a result, some scholars (for example, Beeghley, 2003) consider interactionism to be more akin to social psychology than sociology. Though we do not share this view, there can be little doubt that the adherents of this approach, by concentrating on the interactions between individuals, venture into a territory where psychological dynamics play a very important role. However, unlike their compeers in the psychological disciplines, these scholars' toolbox can boast few of the skills needed to deal with these dynamics adequately (for a theoretical approach to lethal violence whose foundations are largely psycologogical, see for example Prabha Unnithan, Huff-Corzine, Corzine, & Whitt, 1994).

Over above the points of contact and the limitations of the perspectives presented here, it must be emphasized that developing an exhaustive theoretical framework for homicide is a particularly complex task, given the phenomenon's oft-mentioned multidimensionality and extreme heterogeneity. Each perspective contributes to shedding light on a different plane of analysis, and on one type of homicide rather than another. Murderous episodes can vary enormously, and are thus difficult to explain with a single approach. The dynamics of a murder involving two members of rival drug cartels who are personally unacquainted with each other are very different from those characterizing a femicide perpetrated by an obsessively jealous husband, which then differ from those of a parricide following a father's refusal to comply with a drug-addicted son's umpteenth demand for cash. The latter case, in turn, is a far cry from a homicide resulting when a barroom brawl between two people who barely know each other spins out of control. The interactionist perspective, as we have seen, is poorly equipped to explain homicides between strangers belonging to the world of organized crime, or those motivated by economic rather than personal reasons. By contrast, strain theory has long focused on bloodshed in pursuit of financial benefits, given that the socially prescribed goals were largely identified with access to wealth and material wellbeing. Combining the perspectives, rather than embracing only one and denying the other's utility, is all the more necessary in view of the fact that homicide is a much more heterogeneous phenomenon than other forms of criminal behavior.

Lastly, it should be noted that, with the notable exception of Sutherland's work on white collar crime, the theoretical frameworks presented here shed light on the dynamics explaining homicide rates among the deprived segments of the population. This is certainly true for the structuralist and culturalist approaches, but it also holds for the interactionist perspective: the situational elements and interactional dynamics described by Luckenbill clearly apply more to the lower social classes than to those higher on the scale, and the same can be said of the social experiences undergone by dangerous criminals, that Athens argues are at the root of the violentization process. But the reasons that lead the well-off classes to commit murder are still far from clear. Little or no theoretical attention has been devoted to the sociocultural aspects of these episodes, as the dominant thinking centers on the individual elements, regarded from the psychological or psychiatric standpoint. One area that has been neglected by sociological theory, for example, is that of corporate crimes which endanger the lives of workers or the inhabitants of the area surrounding the business. This is a theoretical strand of research that should be addressed in the coming years.

REFERENCES

Agnew, R. (1992). Foundation for a General Strain Theory of Crime and Deliquency. *Criminology*, *30*(1), 47-88.

Agnew, R. (2001). Strain Theory. In E. McLaughlin & J. Muncie (Eds.), *The Sage Dictionary of Criminology*. London: Sage.

Alexander, J. C. & Thompson, K. (2008). *A Contemporary Introduction to Sociology: Culture and Society in Transition*. Boulder: Paradigm Publishers.

Anderson, N. (1923). *The Hobo: The Sociology of the Homeless Man*. Chicago: University Of Chicago Press.

Athens, L. (1980). *Violent Criminal Acts and Actors: A Symbolic Interactionist Study*. Boston: Routledge Kegan & Paul.

Athens, L. (1989). *The Creation of Dangerous Violent Criminals*. London & New York: Routledge.

Barbagli, M., Colombo, A. & Savona, E. (2003). *Sociologia della devianza*. Bologna: Il Mulino.

Bartollas, C. (1985). *Juvenile Deliquency*. New York: MacMillan.

Bean, P. (1990). Reviewed Work: The Creation of Dangerous Violent Criminals by L. H. Athens. *The British Journal of Criminology*, *30*(4), 528-529.

Becker, H. S. (1963). *Outsiders: Studies in the Sociology of Deviance*. New York: Free Press.

Becker, H. S. (1974). Labeling Theory Reconsidered. In P. Rock & M. Mclntoch (Eds.), *Deviance and Social Control* (pp. 41-66). London: Tavistock.

Beeghley, L. (2003). *Homicide. A Sociological Explanation*. Lanham: Rowman & Littlefield Publishers.

Blumer, H. (1969). *Symbolic Interactionism: Perspective and Method*. Englewood Cliffs: Prentice-Hall.

Brookman. (2005). *Understanding Homicide*. London: Sage.

Burgess, E. W. (1925). The Growth of the City. In R. E. Park, E. W. Burgess & D. R. McKenzie (Eds.), *The City*. Chicago: University of Chicago Press.

Burraston, B., Watts, S. J., McCutcheon, C. & Province, K. (2019). Relative Deprivation, Absolute Deprivation, and Homicide: Testing an Interaction Between Income Inequality and Disadvantage. *Homicide Studies*, *23*(1), 3-19.

Bursik, JR. R. J. (1988). Social Disorganization and Theories of Crime and Delinquency: Problems and Prospects. *Criminology*, *26*(4), 519-552.

Cloward, R. A. & Ohlin, L. E. (1960). *Delinquency and Opportunity. A Theory of Delinquent Gangs*. New York: Free Press.

Cohen, A. K. (1955). *Delinquent Boys. The Culture of the Gangs*. New York: Free Press.

Cooley, C. H. (1902). *Human Nature and the Social Order*. New York: C. Scribner's sons.

Corzine, J., Huff-Corzine, L. & Whitt, H. P. (1999). Cultural and Subcultural Theories of Homicide. In M. D. Smith & M. A. Zahn (Eds.), *Homicide. A Sourcebook of Social Research*. Thousand Oaks: Sage.

Cressey, D. R. (1964). Differential Associations and Compulsive Crimes. In D. R. Cressey (Ed.), *Delinquency, Crime and Differential Association*, (pp. 90-107). Dordrecht: Springer Netherlands.

Durkheim, E. (1897). *Suicide*. New York: Free Press (1966).

Elliott, D. S., Ageton, S. S. & Canter, R. J. (1979). An Integrated Theoretical Perspective on Delinquent Behavior. *Journal of Research in Crime and Delinquency*, *16*(1), 3-27.

Erikson, K. (1966). *Wayward Puritans: A Study in the Sociology of Deviance*. New York: John Wiley and Sons.

Goffman, E. (1963a). *Behavior in Public Places: Notes on the Social Organization of Gatherings*. Glencoe: Free press.

Goffman, E. (1963b). *Stigma. Notes on the Management of Spoiled Identity*. Englewood Cliffs: Prentice-Hall.

Goffman, E. (1967). *Interaction Ritual: Essays on Face-to-Face Behavior*. Garden City: Doubleday.

Goffman, E. (1969). *Strategic Interaction*. New York: Ballantine.

Hirschi, T. (1969). *Causes of Deliquency*. Berkeley: University of California Press.

Kitsuse, J. & Cicourel, A. V. (1963). A Note on the Use of Official Statistics. *Social Problems*, *11*(2), 131-139.

Lemert, E. M. (1967). *Human Deviance, Social Problems, and Social Control*. Englewood Cliffs: Prentice-Hall.

Luckenbill, D. F. (1977). Criminal Homicide as a Situated Transaction. *Social Problems*, *25*(2), 176-186.

Lyman, S. & Scott, M. B. (1970). *A Sociology of the Absurd*. New York: Meredith.

Marshall, T. H. (1950). *Citizenship and Social Class*. Cambridge: Cambridge University Press.

Matza, D. (1969). *Becoming Deviant*. Englewood Cliffs: Prentice Hall.

Mead, G. (1934). *Mind, Self, and Society*. Chicago: Chicago University Press.

Merton, R. K. (1938). Social Structure and Anomie. *American Sociological Rev iew*, *3*(5), 672-682.

Messner, S. F. & Rosenfeld, R. (1999). Social Structure and Homicide. In M. D. Smith & M. A. Zahn (Eds.), *Homicide: A Sourcebook of Social Research*. Thousand Oaks: Sage.

Miethe, T. D. & Regoeczi, W. C. (2004). *Rethinking Homicide: Exploring the Structure and Process Underlying Deadly Situations*. Cambridge: Cambridge University Press.

Milovanovic, D. (1996). Postmodern Criminology: Mapping the Terrain. *Justice Quarterly*, *13*(4), 567-609.

Milovanovic, D. (Ed.). (1997). *Chaos, Criminology and Social Justice: The New Orderly (Dis)Order*. Westport: Prager.

Nye, F. I. (1958). *Family Relationships and Delinquent Behavior*. New York: Wiley.

Park, R. E., Burgess, E. W. & McKenzie, D. R. (1925). *The City*. Chicago: University of Chicago Press.

Prabha Unnithan, N., Huff-Corzine, L., Corzine, J. & Whitt, H. P. (1994). *The Currents of Lethal Violence: An Integrated Model of Suicide and Homicide*. New York: State University of New York Press.

Prina, F. (2019). *Devianza e criminalità. Concetti, metodi di ricerca, cause, politiche*. Roma: Carocci.

Radford, J. & Russell, D. E. H. (Eds.). (1992). *Femicide: The Politics of Woman Killing*. Philadelphia: Open University Press.

Reckless, W. C. (1955). *The Crime Problem*. New York: Appleton-Century-Crofts.

Reiss, A. J. jr. (1951). Delinquency as the Failure of Personal and Social Controls. *American Sociological Review*, *16*(2), 196-207.

Rhodes, R. (2000). *Why They Kill; The Discoveries of a Maverick Criminologist*. New York: Vintage.

Rock, P. (2002). Sociological Theories of Crime. In M. Maguire, R. Morgan & R. Reiner (Eds.), *The Oxford Handobook of Criminology (3rd Edition)*. Oxford: Oxford University Press.

Sampson, R. J. & Groves, W. B. (1989). Community Structure and Crime: Testing Social-Disorganization Theory. *American Journal of Sociology, 94*(4), 774-802.

Sampson, R. J. & Laub, J. (1993). *Crime in the Making: Pathways and Turning Points Through Life*. Cambridge: Harvard University Press.

Sellin, T. (1938). *Culture Conflict and Crime*. New York: Social Science Research Council.

Shaw, C. R. (1929). *Deliquency Areas*. Chicago: The University of Chicago Press.

Shaw, C. R. & McKay, H. D. (1942). *Juvenile Delinquency and Urban Areas: A Study of Rates of Delinquents in Relation to Differential Characteristics of Local Communities in American Cities*. Chicago: The University of Chicago Press.

Sutherland, E. H. (1939). *Principles of Criminology* Philadelphia: Lippincott.

Sutherland, E. H. (1949). *White Collar Crime*. New York: Holt, Rinehart & Winston.

Swidler, A. (1986). Culture in Action: Symbols and Strategies. *American Sociological Review, 51*(2), 273-286.

Sykes, G. M. & Matza, D. (1957). Techniques of Neutralization: A Theory of Delinquency. *American Sociological Review, 22*(6), 664-670.

Thomas, W. I. & Znaniecki, F. (1920). *The Polish Peasant in Europe and America*. Boston: The Gorham Press.

Toby, J. A. (1957). Social Disorganization and Stake in Conformity: Complementary Factors in the Predatory Behavior of Hoodlums. *Journal of Criminal Law & Criminology, 48*(1), 12-17.

Von Hentig, H. (1948). *The Criminal and His Victim*. New Haven: Yale University Press.

Williams, F. P. & McShane, M. D. (1994). *Criminological Theory*. Englewood Cliffs: Prentice Hall.

Wirth, L. (1931). Culture Conflict and Delinquency. I. Culture Conflict and Misconduct. *Social Forces*, 9(4), 484-492.

Wolfgang, M. E. (1958). *Patterns in Criminal Homicide*. Philadelphia: University of Pennsylvania Press.

Wolfgang, M. E. & Ferracuti, F. (1967). *The Subculture of Violence: Towards an Integrated Theory in Criminology*. London: Tavistock.

In: Advances in Sociology Research ISBN: 978-1-53616-781-8
Editor: Jared A. Jaworski © 2020 Nova Science Publishers, Inc.

Chapter 2

REVISITING MIGRATION CRISIS IN GREECE: STAKEHOLDERS IN DIALOGUE: INTEGRATION STRATEGIES IN THE FIELD OF HEALTHCARE AND SOCIAL CARE AT NATIONAL LEVEL

George Koulierakis[1], Elisavet Ioannidi[1],
Paraskevi Gikopoulou[1], Maria Psoinos[1], Ilse Derluyn[2],
Nora Perdu[2], Maria Moudatsou[3], Stefania Pantazi[3],
Eleni Dimopoulou[3], Tania Tsiakou[3],
Theodoros Fouskas[4], Andrea de Maio[4], Pavlos Stefanou[4],
Despina-Electra Voulgari[4], Konstantinos Kazanas[4],
Fotini-Maria Mine[4], Vasiliki Tsigka[4], Georgia Pechlidi[4],
Anastasios Mastroyiannakis[5], Caroline Antunes[5],
Maria Poulopoulou[5], Nikos Gionakis[6]
and Marianna Asimakopoulou[6]

[1]Department of Public Health Policy, University of West Attica,
Athens, Greece
[2]University of Ghent, Ghent, Belgium
[3]NGO PRAKSIS, Athens, Greece

[4]European Public Law Organisation, Athens, Greece
[5]CMT PROOPTIKI, Athens, Greece
[6]Syn-Eirmos, Athens, Greece

ABSTRACT

Since 2015, the European continent confronts an unprecedented migration influx that has triggered humanitarian crisis. Years later, the first waves of uprooted populations are seeking integration in the host countries, while Greece is setting up viable national strategies so as to integrate Third Country Nationals (TCNs). This chapter presents the first research findings of the EU funded project *Local Alliance for Integration* (accr. LION) in the field of healthcare and social care at a national level. It draws upon the empirical findings of one focus group with local stakeholders in the field of healthcare and social care in order to address the needs of TCNs and reveals the existing challenges. The qualitative research took place in Athens and centres around the integration policies in the field of healthcare and social care under the methodological prism and review of best practices at EU and national level (Greece). It is argued that there are still some measures to be taken in order to cover adequately the healthcare and social care needs of TCNs, such as intercultural mediation and interpreting in the Greek National Health System (NHS); information provision regarding the healthcare rights of the newcomers; strengthening the housing policy and maintaining funds for vulnerable groups such as unaccompanied minors, victims of torture, Gender-Based Violence (GBV) and Sexual and Gender-Based Violence (SGBV) survivors; a well-designed integration plan at a national level; and stronger coordination between the Greek State and non-state organisations. In conclusion, even though the crisis days are past behind us, the country - in many parts - is still struggling at the level of emergency.

1. INTRODUCTION

According to the World Health Organization (WHO), there are many differences between the European member states regarding both healthcare and social care services and strategies for Third Country Nationals (TCNs) (WHO, 2018). Greece has been one of those countries facing many challenges in the field of migration. Over the past few years and especially in the aftermath of 2015 migrant/refugee influx, several programmes were implemented in Greece, in order to deal with the emergency situation of the new populations who were seeking family-reunification, EU relocation and asylum seeking within the European Union. Indicatively, from 2015 onwards, Medecins Sans Frontieres (MSF) in Greece, among many other organisations and rescue teams, participated in the rescue of more than 20,000 migrants and refugees in the Mediterranean and Aegean Seas (msf.gr). According to the United Nations High Commissioner for Refugees (UNHCR) data, Greece saw 62% increase of migrant flows in 2018, while only in the months of February, March and April of 2018, the country recorded 8,362 new sea arrivals. In practical terms, the latter accords with 162% increase of migrants compared to 2017 records (UNHCR, 2018a).

This chapter considers the needs of TCNs that are currently observed in the Greek society, by examining and identifying a number of *best practices* in the field of healthcare and social care at EU level, providing a comparative outlook as a reference point. It then contextualizes the EU policies in national terms, namely Greece, stressing upon primary and mental healthcare, the current social services that are available in the field of social care, as well as the provision of care to vulnerable groups such as Sexual and Gender-Based Violence (SGBV) survivors, LGBTQI+ populations, and unaccompanied minors, as well as the barriers and problems in the Greek arena. This overall discussion is furnished by rich qualitative data collected through a focus group comprised of public officials and NGO representatives, in order to simultaneously explain the needs and shortcomings. The need to accommodate vulnerable populations is especially discussed in this chapter, for it was estimated according to 2018 figures that 3,400 unaccompanied refugee minors were somewhere dispersed in Greece; only 1,101 of them had secured shelter, while the remaining 2,569 were still out of shelter with their applications pending. Out of these numbers, 692 minors were reported "homeless" and 409 missing (Centre for Social Solidarity, EKKA, 2018; see also Hatzopoulos et al., 2018). Regarding housing, the UNHCR introduced a new accommodation scheme implemented under Emergency Support to Integration and Accommodation (ESTIA) programme (and funded by ECHO) in order to cover 24,500 accommodation spaces throughout Greece (UNHCR, 2018a, May 28; UNHCR 2018b, May 30).

It is of a vital importance to mention that the Greek State soon implements an integration plan at national level in order to give priority to the "homeless" children and strengthen the housing policy in Greece as a whole. NGOs are currently responsible for meeting housing needs to vulnerable populations, as we already argued (for more information regarding the situation of refugee minors and shelters in Greece see PRAKSIS' National Report of 2018 at www.praksis.gr/en/). However, the unprecedented scale of migrant influx left many minors out of building structures exposed to danger as the qualitative analysis will show in this chapter. In addition, the limited funding at a state level (amid financial crisis) regarding accommodation is juxtaposed with the country's legal obligation towards certain vulnerable groups of migrants. Article 19 (2) of the Presidential Decree No.220/2007 renders "authorities responsible for accommodation" and presupposes that "unaccompanied minors are placed with adult relatives or a foster family, in accommodation centres with special provision for minors, and are protected from trafficking or exploitation" (WHO, 2015, p. 9).

At the same time, a chain of amended immigration acts in many EU countries affected the resettlement policies for thousands of unaccompanied minors, leaving them stranded in countries such as Greece, Italy and France. It is mainly the latter countries that have received the highest number of unaccompanied minors. According to the *Guardian,* Greece had approximately 3,300 unaccompanied minors (based on December 2017 figures), while Italy had 13,867, and 11,186 in France (Taylor, 2017, December 15; see also Sparrow, 2017, December 22; Ministry for Migration Policy/Asylum Service, 2018b; Ministry for Migration Policy/Asylum Service 2018c). The current situation was exacerbated due to the shift in the UK Immigration Bill under the notorious

Dubs[1] scheme in 2016, which initially foresaw the resettlement of at least 3,000 unaccompanied minors from the most affected EU countries to UK shelters (Home Office, 2016). UK Immigration Bill agreed in the end to transfer only 480 unaccompanied refugees from Europe, and just 50 from Greece, drafting at the same time difficult eligibility criteria in the notorious *BID report* (Safe Passage UK and PRAKSIS, 2017, March 17). Last but not least, this chapter closes by discussing both weaknesses and challenges of the current integration policies in Greece, in order to bring forth suggestive ways to improve and upgrade the current integration mechanisms for TCNs.

2. INTEGRATION POLICY AT EU LEVEL

To begin with the European context that provides the basis of the discussion around the theme of integration of TCNs, the EU integration policy of TCNs is directed by the recast reception Directive 2013/33/EU which states that EU 'Member States shall ensure that material reception conditions provide an adequate standard of living for applicants for international protection, which guarantees their subsistence and protects their physical and mental health'. It furthermore states that 'Member States shall ensure that the standard of living is met in the specific situation of vulnerable persons, in accordance with Article 21, as well as in relation to the situation of persons who are in detention. Member States may make the provision of all or some of the material reception conditions and health care subject to the condition that applicants do not have sufficient means to have a standard of living adequate for their health and to enable their subsistence' (Art. 17, par. 2,3). Under this legal canon, equal access to healthcare in the host country is granted to asylum seekers, refugees, and persons under subsidiary protection on the same grounds as all other citizens (art. 30 of Directive 2011/95/EU).

---

[1] Named after Labour MP Lord Baron Dubs.

3. CONTEXTUALISING THE INTEGRATION POLICY IN GREECE

With regards to the integrationist model of migrants'[2] healthcare and social care at Greek level, the prognosis is grim. The most comprehensive work that best describes the current situation in Greece was published by the International Organization for Migration (IOM) in 2016, revealing the lack of any method and/or policy on health integration and social care of migrants (IOM, 2016). The above study reviewed migrants of 38 EU/EFTA countries including North Macedonia and Turkey, aiming at addressing comparatively the EU policy on health integration. The study suggested that no Greek government had acted upon or published any measures regarding migrant health policy, even though the country has attracted funded research on health policy so as to address migrants' health and social care needs (IOM, 2016). However, IOM's MIPEX revealed that TCNs have not been included - so far - in any study, and medical staff has not received "professional education" or training in order to meet the former's special needs (IOM, 2016, p. 70).

Moreover, a 2018 study published on the European Web Site of the EU Commission *on Migrant Integration Information and good practices*, described analogous trends on the Greek front, as it realizes that there is no "health strategy targeting migrants", "integration strategy targeting health", "standards on cultural mediators", "free interpreters", or "health indicators for migrants" (Mikaba, 2018). The current (2019) socio-political situation in the country is by no means an exclusive Greek problem; on the contrary, it aligned with the European banking crisis of 2008 that led to severe budget cuts in the health sector, along with the rise of populist, far right and anti-immigration political parties and factions throughout EU, which aggravated the problem (Mladovsky, et al., 2012; see also Papadaki et al., 2017). Without a policy of integration, provision of healthcare and social care of TCNs renders impossible; hence, unequal access to health and

---

2 The term migrant refers to all people on the move and with different legal statuses (IOM, 2019). However, for the purposes of the current research, the integration policy does not include undocumented migrants.

absence of integration policy not only co-exist, but presuppose one another without contradictions: *"International and European frameworks pave the way for health equity but no equal access to health care is possible without national commitments. National legislations, policies and actions are therefore required to comply with international and European standards that set parameters for the respect of human rights[3], including health"* (Mikaba, 2018).

From 2015 until now, there have been at least 48,000 migrants displaced within mainland Greece and in the islands (Skleparis, 2018). Even though there are binding international protection laws that guarantee free access to healthcare for TCNs in Greece, the wrecked economy ravaged medical supplies and drugs, shrunk the number of medical practitioners, but also the number of female physicians, revealed the absence of interpreters within hospitals, while medical examinations are not always free of charge (Skleparis, 2018). All these challenges have summoned Greece to take action on a firm and just integration policy based on EU laws. This was not an easy task, given the debt-stricken health system of the country. Since 2016, new efforts were made on the basis of collaboration between the Greek State and the World Health Organisation (WHO) in order to strengthen "financial sustainability of the health system", boost "modernization of health coverage", and "enhancing universal access to quality care" (WHO, 2016). At the same time, the state recently introduced a new health programme for migrants and refugees in the islands, recruiting so far 200 health professionals so as to invigorate busy hospitals (Boussias, 2018). The latter argument epitomises once more that integration policy is pending when the country still works at the level of emergency. Moreover, the European Union published a paper that summarises the views of the Europeans with reference to the integration of TCNs. Regarding the latter, the EU barometer revealed that around 68% of the Greek population believes that poor access to health care "is a major obstacle" towards integration (European Commission, 2018, p. 104). In contrast, and according to WHO, "support for integration … is associated

---

3 The right to health is a fundamental human right as adopted in article 12 of the UN's General Assembly (UN General Assembly, 1966).

with better health outcomes" (Bradby, et al., 2015, p. x). To improve health outcomes in turn, it has been declared that more stress must be put on "developing innovative and sustained strategies" on matters of healthcare and screening not just at EU level, but within research communities and policy makers as well (Seedat, et al., 2018, p. 1).

However, in 2016, the Greek State passed new legislation (Law 4368/2016, art. 33), which allows all citizens of the country including TCNs to apply for a social security number (AMKA)[4], thus paving the way towards free access to the Greek National Health System. This by all means has socio-legal gravity, as Law 4368/2016 binds the Greek State to insure all TCNs on exactly the same legal grounds as the rest of the Greek population, and for that matter the IOM published a paper that provides information as to how to apply the law to medical practice (IOM, 2017). Under the same rationale, the European Commission, stressed upon the significance of promoting "equal access to primary health care" especially with respect to "maternal health" at EU level as well as Greek level. To do so, it has been argued that, "the recruitment of bilingual health workers, medical and care providers [...] would be in position to better meet migrant women's needs"; hence, the latter reveals that migrant patients are often unaware of their health rights (European Web Site on Integration, 2017b, October 6).

The right to equal access to healthcare is challenging; in the past, there have been allegations, whereby migrants' AMKA applications were denied without justification despite holding all sufficient requirements and this issue attracted EC attention (European Web Site on Integration, 2017a, August 3). The European Commission published in 2016 a unified and cohesive plan for all EU member states in order to design an integration policy that will tackle issues of housing, employment, education and of course access to free health care. Additionally, the latter *Action Plan* of the EU Commission binds the countries with grants to support TCNs to become active and equal members of local societies, meeting basic needs. At the same time, the EU-funds, support "best practices in health provision

---

4 AMKA stands for Arithmos Mitroou Koinonikis Asfalisis (Social Security Number).

for vulnerable individuals especially refugees" (European Commission, 2016, p. 11; see also European Migration Network, 2017).

Before identifying and analysing best practices at EU level and in Greece in the field of healthcare and social care, it is crucial first to give a definition.

4. BEST PRACTICES: TOWARDS A DEFINITION

Best practices serve as a useful guiding tool in order to identify the needs of society, whether those relate to immigration as a whole, certain aspect of it, or social phenomena at large (Portugal et al., 2007). In doing so, best practices provide a special *modus operandi* and the foundation for a model of general principles, one of which is according to Portugal et al. (2007), the *UNESCO* model that has been adopted for the present purpose by the LION Project (Psoinos et al., 2016).

This model of best practices however is not exhaustive (EN-HERA!, 2009). The *UNESCO* model of best practices has the following four parameters:

1. *Best practices are innovative.* A best practice has developed new and creative solutions to common problems that are consequence of immigration, poverty and social exclusion.
2. *Best practices make a difference.* A best practice demonstrates a positive and tangible impact on the living conditions, quality of life or environment of the individuals, groups or communities concerned.
3. *Best practices have a sustainable effect.* A best practice contributes to sustained eradication of poverty or social exclusion, especially by the involvement of participants.
4. *Best practices have the potential for replication.* A best practice serves as a model for generating policies and initiatives elsewhere.

5. BEST PRACTICES AT EU LEVEL

Identifying best practices at EU level presupposes a common ground for implementing healthcare standards to TCNs and acts as a prelude towards identifying strategies at a national level. Below there is a brief analysis of indicative best practices that have been identified at EU level and can be used as a guiding tool for Greece.

The HPH Task Force on Migration, Equity & Diversity (Taskforce MED) (www.hphnet.org/copy-of-tf-and-wg-1), for instance can be considered as a good practice related to integration in health care. TF MED was introduced in December 2016 aiming at supporting organisations to establish policies where provision and healthcare would be accessible to TCNs. At the same time, it monitors the effective implementation by developing and pilot testing in several countries a set of Standards for Equity in health care (Chiarenza et al. 2014).

Monitoring of health status constitutes another good practice which was used in the context of CARE-project (www.careformigrants.eu) by creating an integrated electronic system for tracking and monitoring the health status of migrants and refugees in line with IOM's Personal Health Record (CARE, 2017). The previous mentioned system included training legal personnel and medical and non-medical staff.

Another good practice at EU level in the field of healthcare is the EQUI-HEALTH which was first introduced in February 2013 by the Migration Health Division of the Regional Office for Europe of IOM (eea.iom.int/equi-health). EQUI-HEALTH implements training programmes such as "The Training of Trainers (ToT) package" focusing on educating healthcare and legal staff on matters migration, border management, and health and cultural competence.

6. BEST PRACTICES IN GREECE

6.1. Healthcare and Social Care

Moving onto Greece, a past action that met the above criteria and could be considered a 'good practice' in the field of healthcare was the vaccination campaign that occurred in 2016 (Psoinos et al., 2016). The design and coordination of the programme was carried out by the Ministry of Health and the National Public Health Organization (NPHO) (f. KEELPNO); the programme was implemented by the Ministry of Health, in collaboration with major NGOs, such as MSF, MDM, Red Cross, PRAKSIS and many municipalities, that offered to NGOs extra spaces, such as the municipal clinics, in order to implement the programme. This common initiative not only targeted the vaccination of migrant/refugee children in major hosting structures, but also targeted assessment and prevention. At the same time, the vaccination programme brought together different organisations and state institutions, proving that collaboration and networking was possible and could be actualised in an exemplary way. In addition, the National Health Operations Centre (EKEPY) [5] , in collaboration with the Ministry of Health, undertook the role of surveilling the whole procedure and supervising NGOs in the field, while all state and non-state parties were exchanging information regarding the smooth operation of the programme (i.e., the progress of referrals, medical appointments, discussion and follow-up of strengths and weaknesses). The vaccination programme remains intact and the NPHO publishes weekly reports as to the migrants-refugee's epidemiological surveillance (https: //philosgreece.eu/en/informative-material/epidemiological-surveillance).
At the same time, EKEPY still operates in the camps and continues to collaborate with the Ministry of Health along with many NGOs since 2015.

The above mentioned best practices refer more to the management of crisis rather than integration as such. However, those mentioned below adhere to the four criteria of best practices and could be used for the forthcoming agenda of integration in the field of healthcare and social care.

---

5 EKEPY stands for Ethniko Kentro Epixeiriseon Ygeias (National Health Operations Centre).

Thus, regarding best practices in Greece, it is of a vital importance to secure a sustained model of healthcare on a statist ground that goes beyond the mere call of meeting the basic needs of migrants/refugees; it should also encompass the issue of social care and mental well-being, for the social provision is currently and almost exclusively at the hands of NGOs.

One example of good practice that satisfies the *sustainability*, *replication*, and *innovation* in the field of social and mental care, is the work of BABEL Day Centre for Migrants (syn-eirmos.gr). BABEL Day Centre is the only mental care service that sprung from the Greek State's initiative twelve years ago. It runs since 2007 and is considered a solid foundation for meeting migrants/ refugees' social and mental needs. Over the past twelve years, BABEL focuses on psychosocial support and provides assistance to people from all walks of life; to those who lost their residency, their right to have a country, and to those who became uprooted, receiving care irrespective of national, cultural, religious, ethnic and socio-economic background (Gkionakis, 2016).

Within the same rationale, there are other NGOs – pioneers in the Greek arena – such as PRAKSIS (www.praksis.gr/en/) that provides direct and primary health care and pharmaceutical provision, basic hygiene services, psychosocial support, job counselling, legal counselling, side supportive services, accommodation facilities, and interpretation to all vulnerable groups. PRAKSIS' programmes aim at combating socio-economic exclusion of vulnerable and marginalized groups, such as impoverished Greek population, homeless, uninsured, economic migrants, asylum seekers, refugees, unaccompanied and separated children, SGBV,GBV, trafficking survivors, victims of torture, sex workers, children begging in the streets, vulnerable youth, injection drug users, Roma, HIV seropositive people/PLWHA, Hepatitis B and C patients, LGBTQI+, prisoners and ex-prisoners. PRAKSIS' work is geared towards a holistic approach aiming at assisting migrants, refugees, and socially excluded populations not only at the level of psychosocial support and health provision, but also at the level of integration.

PRAKSIS' humanitarian work, like BABEL's Day Centre is considered a good practice not only on the basis of innovation, and sustainability, but on the grounds that it makes a difference and can be replicable; to the extent that it can serve as a model of integration to TCNs and a means of pressure towards the State, so as to encourage analogous efforts to flourish all over Greece. PRAKSIS Youth Shelter, for instance, was created precisely on the basis of this need: to create a shelter for refugees who became adults and needed a transition period in order to integrate in the Greek sociopolitical fabric (Karavaltsiou, 2017). The constant presence of PRAKSIS in the field of healthcare and social care would have rendered impossible without the continuous cooperation of other major NGOs that fund and enable the sustainability of the programmes, strengthening at the same time collaboration.

Apart from PRAKSIS, there are the NGOs ARSIS (www.arsis.gr) and CARITAS HELLAS (www.caritas.gr), that focus on the integration of TCNs in the Greek society, offering social support and of course housing. NGO ARSIS for instance, runs shelters for refugee families, unaccompanied minors and single parent families in many parts of Greece, while CARITAS HELLAS implements housing programmes co-funded by CARITAS Germany and the German Foreign Office.

Furthermore, it is worth to mention the work of the Greek Forum for Refugees (GFR) (refugees.gr/), and the Greek Council for Refugees (GCR) (www.gcr.gr/el/). The latter operates since 1989, with branches in the islands, mainland Greece, as well as Athens and Thessaloniki. They focus on psychosocial support, offering information and advice regarding housing, emergency management, education, and employment. In addition, GCR has a long tradition of legal aid, as the latter constitutes an integral part and a pre-condition towards integration. The Greek Forum for Refugees on the other hand, seeks to raise awareness, focuses upon TCNs' active participation in the Greek Society, transferring their opinions into the Greek Parliament. A similar online platform that offers social, medical, legal advice and information to TCN's, has been created by the website *SafeRefugees* (www.saferefugees.info/greek-main).

6.2. Networks of Collaboration in the Field of Healthcare and Social Care

Collaboration between many different stakeholders plays a pivotal role in establishing the fertile ground for implementing best practices. Apart from the vaccination campaign of 2015, that constitutes until today a boisterous example of collaboration and a good practice between the Ministry of Health and non-state institutions, it is perhaps important to argue that the presence of UNHCR Greece (www.unhcr.org/gr/), proved to be catalytic with regards to funding local and international NGOs in order to enable and sustain their humanitarian work. At the same time, UNHCR Greece collaborates with the state on issues of integration, health, housing, social care, education etc. Some of the partners are PRAKSIS, ARSIS, METAdrasi, FAROS, Mercy Corps, Network for the Rights of Children, IFRC, EPAPSY, Solidarity Now, Doctors of the World, *Diotima*, Greek Council for the Refugees, INTERSOS, FAROS, KEAN, as well as many municipalities throughout Greece.

Furthermore, there is another national establishment – the National Centre for Social Solidarity (EKKA)[6] - that collaborates with a plethora of NGOs in the field of social care and housing. EKKA, in collaboration with UNICEF, processes numerous applications of unaccompanied refugee children per month, in order for them to be granted shelter, and has become the mediator between the Asylum Service and NGOs (WHO, 2015; see also Ministry for Migration Policy/Asylum Service, 2018a).

7. INTERCULTURAL MEDIATION IN THE HEALTHCARE AND SOCIAL CARE SECTOR

Intercultural mediation constitutes an integral part in the field of healthcare and social care for TCNs. At a national level, there is no policy yet that foresees the recruitment of highly trained interpreters within hospitals so as to enable proper consultation between medical staff and

---

6 EKKA stands for Ethniko Kentro Koinonikis Allileguis (National Centre of Social Solidarity).

migrant/refugee patients. At an NGO level, however, there are many organisations where intercultural mediation is a precondition and a means towards integration. Apart from those already listed above, METAdrasi (metadrasi.org/en/home) is an example of intercultural efficiency *par excellence*, and a best practice to serve as an integrationist model on national grounds. For seven years now, METAdrasi not only focuses on medical and social provision, but also invests greatly upon intercultural mediation within hospitals. Highly trained personnel and volunteers are constantly present within medical premises throughout Greece consisting of 350 interpreters fluent in 43 languages and dialects that collaborate with major Hospitals in order to assist TCNs. At the level of state however, the scarcity of interpreters in the Greek NHS prevents medical staff to really address migrants' health needs; hence, lack of intercultural mediation conserves health rights unawareness from the part of TCNs. Without intercultural efficiency and representation within Public Hospitals, proper consultation renders impossible for TCNs (Marouda, et al., 2014). Given the absence of interpreters at national level, EKEPY collaborated in the past with NGOs in the camps in order for the latter to assist them with interpreters. At the same time, EKEPY in partnership with the Ministry of Health (via PHILOS Programme)[7], organises trainings since 2017 in order to inform NGOs as to the Gender-Based Violence (GBV) protocol, along with many other issues such as finding the means to purchase specific medication (National Health Operations Centre, EKEPY, 2017a).

Having in mind the theoretical review which encompassed this chapter so far and after discussing best practices at EU and national level in the field of healthcare and social care, there follows a qualitative analysis of one focus group. The remaining section of this chapter unfolds at empirical level and in concrete terms the healthcare and social care needs of TCNs in Greece by the indispensable contribution and knowledge of local stakeholders who are experts in the field of migration and refugee crisis. Prior to the analysis of the qualitative findings however, the methodology section that is provided just below, explains the logic and scope of the focus group.

---

7 https://philosgreece.eu/en/home/about.

8. METHODOLOGY

The methodology of this chapter belongs to a rich qualitative research project that was crafted for the implementation of the EU programme called Local Alliance for Integration (accr. LION) (www.alliance-forintegration.eu), which has received funding from the European Union's Asylum, Migration and Integration Fund (AMIF-2016-AG-INTE 2017-2019). This chapter has abstracted only one part of the analysed research findings of the programme, including the literature review on the identification of best practices at EU level and national level (Greece) in concert with the qualitative analysis of one focus group.

The focus group took place in Athens, Greece, on 16 March 2018, at the Department of Public Health Policy, University of West Attica. The primary objective of the focus group was to address the needs and challenges in the field of healthcare and social care in order suggest solutions with regards to the integration policy in Greece. Nine (9) participants took part in the focus group. The latter was composed by officials from the Greek Ministry of Health, the National Public Health Organization (NPHO), the Médecins Sans Frontières (MSF), the International Rescue Committee (IRC), the Society of Social Psychiatry and Mental Health (EKPE), the Spanish Red Cross (SRC), the BABEL (Day Centre for Migrant's Mental Health – Syn-Eirmos), the Association for Regional Development and Mental Health (EPAPSY), and the NGO PRAKSIS.

The methodology of the focus group implementation was designed by Ghent University and reviewed by the Department of Public Health Policy, crafting an outline of 24 open-ended questions that targeted the theme of integration (policy, existing practices, networking, suggestions for improvements), in the field of healthcare and social care. Some questions were more general and sketchy, whereas other questions were more explicit and concrete. However, all open-ended questions gave the freedom to the participants to engage into a fruitful discussion and debate on issues around TCNs' integration in the field of healthcare, prevention, social care, and in order to suggest solutions.

The focus group method was approved by the Ethics Committee of the Department of Public Health Policy, at the University of West Attica. Participants were informed about the methods and scope of the focus group, including the right to audio-record and analyse the raw material only by the researchers, assured for the anonymity and the voluntary participation and signed individual informed consent forms. The focus group was audio-recorded and the raw material was literally transcribed.

9. FINDINGS

9.1. Stakeholders in Dialogue

The existing literature reminds us the gaps that are present in Greece in the field of healthcare and social care. The findings from the focus group explain further and in concrete terms a policy of integration which has been well thought but not yet implemented, even though there have been organised actions but not within a unified plan. As one interviewee argued:

> [...] recognising maybe all the positive intentions, positive actions, efforts and so on, I think, personally my assessment is that these are actions that are not integrated into a general planning and frame, and I would like to see a bigger result [...] (Interviewee 2).

Greece received for the first time EU funding to design and implement a strategic plan that is geared towards integrating TCNs in the Greek socio-political fabric. Two programmes started under the auspices of the state: the *PHILOS Programme* (philosgreece.eu/el/home/about), which runs in the islands, kicked off in October 2017, while *Polydynamos Programme* was due to start in July 2018, lasting for approximately two years. The Ministry of Health and the Ministry for Migration Policy set up a "national plan" in order to identify the basic needs of TCNs and put them into praxis. The primary aspect of the Greek policy is to provide and guarantee social security numbers (AMKA) to all refugees who hold registration number, in order to have free access to the NHS. In the islands, for instance, which is the first entry-point of refugees and migrants, the primary objective was to issue social security number the soonest possible, even though currently, there are bureaucratic delays. As one interviewee commented:

> [...] one way is the immediate issue of AMKA for citizens, for all those people provided they are documented by the police (we shouldn't ignore that), and once they hold a registration number, an applicant card as it is called, and so on, then onwards, they have the right to issue AMKA, with all the bureaucratic difficulties this entails, namely, that it is not issued fast or easily, KEP do not issue, [...] but the final goal is this, namely for all those people to issue AMKA, these services to evolve, so as to show them the way towards the NHS (to Hospitals, health centres); There is no other way, and this is implemented [...] (Interviewee 3).

Regarding patients with chronic disease, an example was mentioned, concerning patients with diabetes, indicating that the Ministry of Health pressures the local authorities to issue AMKA as soon as possible with the assistance of social workers of the new programme of PHILOS. The latter would enable beneficiaries to seek medication within the Greek hospitals and local clinics, avoiding the current situation of seeking medication in local 'set-up' pharmacies.

> [...] For a diabetic for example, we pressure to make sure the authorities issue AMKA immediately, so as he/she finds his/her way towards the NHS, so as to skip setting up pharmacies to provide insulin and so on, which is totally wrong within camps. So it is important for these people to acquire AMKA, to find their way towards the NHS, and in turn, the latter must be strengthened. [...] And this is being implemented right now [...] (Interviewee 3).

Furthermore, it has been argued that the integration policy foresees the "removal of ghetto services", the "strengthening of health services", "building up new spaces", and improving the conditions of hygiene.

> [...] basic keystone of which is the removal of ghetto services in the camps and elsewhere, and the strengthening of health structures, so as these people wherever they are, [...] not just for the 60,000, but everyone who lives in the country, and they are refugees /migrants, in order for all to find their way towards the NHS [...] (Interviewee 3).

As stated and up until now, the Greek National Health System did not get involved in the decision making process, nor did the Ministry of Health had an active role as to the quality of the reception centres. As one interviewee noted:

> [...] the Ministry of Health does not participate as it should in the decision making with regards to the reception centres. It is the army, the Ministry of Migration and the EU that has the role on this, that's the truth [...] (Interviewee 3).

By undertaking the new programmes, the Ministry of Health seeks to strengthen the building structures, promote and boost health, focus on "mental health", "health prevention", and "prevention of abuse". Another key aspect of the funded Polydynamos programme as it has been suggested, was that "information desks", (otherwise 'help desks'), and 'intercultural offices' would be set up within hospitals, to act as facilitating mechanisms, guarantying free and easy access to TCNs in the Health System. At a later stage, the intention was to introduce the "registry of intercultural mediation in health" which will establish the role and ethical code of intercultural mediators in hospitals.

> [...] we set up into our hospitals (what other countries have discovered in 1992), namely [...] information desks, help desks, intercultural offices, [...] which started in Italy and the UK, that facilitate citizens to move around the hospital. They do not just translate, but they are intercultural mediators. The basic keystone of the programme [...] is the registry of intercultural mediation in health [...] It is a particular activity, with the primary goal to establish working rights [...] (Interviewee 3).

Another key feature of the programme is geared towards promoting education and training among medical staff and intercultural mediators, strengthening the departments of Gynecology and Midwifery in terms of personnel, and boosting social services within public hospitals. With regards to intercultural mediation and the barriers that are observed within hospitals, it was noted by one interviewee that:

[…] from our minor experience (in relation to people's access to hospitals), is that whenever people are escorted by interpreters, the treatment is very good from the part of the hospitals in Athens; doctors, nurses, and everyone are willing to help. When they are not escorted (and I believe it goes without saying) cannot be understood and they get disappointed as well, for they wait for many hours to be treated and when they do get treated, they visit for a specific reason, but the doctor understands something else […] (Interviewee 5).

At the same time, the Ministry of Health seems to be aware of certain parameters that currently pose obstacles but those are sought to be solved, implementing the actions step by step. Furthermore, the PHILOS programme of the Ministry of Health does not seek to resume their collaboration with the NGOs, exclude them from the field, "supervise" or "monitor" them; on the contrary, it calls for a more organised and coordinated affinity with the latter, in the form of "specialized interventions". More specifically, the Ministry of Health will lead on issues of "direct hospitalisation" and "primary care", and collaborate with specialized NGOs on more sensitive health issues. In other words, the Ministry of Health will re-introduce a new collaboration mechanism between the state and NGOs, as the former cannot substitute the vital work of the latter. It was argued that, the state alone cannot lift the weight of the refugee crisis, especially when certain epidemics spread throughout Greece such as measles, and they need the contribution and experience of NGOs to carry on their vital work. Collaboration will continue as in the past as it was argued, with various organisations such as the Red Cross, Doctors of the World, and MSF on issues of vaccination, and with many other NGOs, experts on the field, on sensitive and special cases. As one interviewee noted:

[…] We collaborate for simpler cases with the Doctors of the World, MSF, with the Red Cross, for the vaccination [...] However, both our expertise and our capabilities cannot handle the majority of refugee population and Roma and so on, especially in the middle of an epidemic such as measles in Greece. […] but others say: NGOs will stop running, we say no to this […], but we change the level of collaboration for sure along with the coordination of the Ministry of Health, not via supervision or monitoring but via coordination and organized […] (Interviewee 3).

Furthermore,

> [...] primary care [...] the responsibility of hospitalization,
> healthcare must be the responsibility of the Ministry of Health, however,
> as to the specialized interventions, cases of torture, mental health,
> mother-child axis, victims of violence and so on, will always be in
> collaboration with specialized NGOs [...] (Interviewee 3).

9.2. Mental Health

With regards to mental health, it has been declared that the opening of
BABEL Day Centre, twelve years ago, with the approval and support of
the State, still constitutes an exemplary case of care. Apart from this
initiative, there have been no other developments at national level, as there
is no other unit from the part of the state that deals with the mental health
of TCNs. When BABEL made its first steps a decade ago, it acted as a
"regulatory agent" for the appropriate reception of new populations. It has
been argued, that more efforts need to be made on the level of structures
and their maintenance, and on the establishment of an open system that
will allow patients - treated for mental issues - refer to other sectors of the
NHS when those needs do not directly address psychopathological
symptoms, but refer to other medical issues. Therefore, BABEL's mission
was to:

> [...] to be a sort of a regulatory agent, namely, to act as mediators,
> for the appropriate reception of these people who come from other
> countries, in public structures. This is a very good plan, if those structures
> exist, and do operate. If I talk about children's mental health, these
> structures do not exist...so where should one refer to? [...] mediate on
> behalf of someone, but to reach who? [...] (Interviewee 8).

The previous argument has raised another parameter which is crucial
in the field of mental health; namely, the information tools TCNs have at
the moment, regarding their accessibility to certain mental and social care
services. It was stressed that, it is significant for migrants to be aware of
the services that are currently available, and learn how to reach the NHS,

including many NGOs alongside BABEL Day Centre, that have capacity buildings, mobile units, day centres and apartments. Thus, emphasis must be given on intercultural mediation as well as on "training the system" to establish links between the NHS and Third Country Nationals. The latter in turn must become familiar with the Greek health system, understand their health rights and become aware of the importance of visiting a physician.

> [...] There are people who never visited the doctor. And when you ask them to go to the doctor, it is like asking them maybe to do something which is outside their culture, especially in the case of a psychiatrist. So, one large part must invest on information, sensitization, and at the level of prevention, and of course here I am not optimistic, because not many things have been done in Greece yet regarding vulnerable groups, therefore, I don't know [...] (Interviewee 5).

9.3. Vulnerable Groups

The previous argument precipitated a chain of other issues during the focus group, one of which was the unresolved issue of housing, especially in the case of vulnerable groups. The latter, indeed raises concerns among NGO personnel and policy makers. During the focus group, it has been argued that there is no actual policy yet that foresees solutions to housing problem at national level. Victims of abuse, GBV survivors, unaccompanied minors, and LGBTQI+ populations do not receive proper care. The only provision that is been offered to vulnerable groups is through NGOs. It was mentioned the unpreparedness of the system to support these people, in terms of identifying them, hosting them in appropriate structures, and confronting with the high accommodation demand, and providing accommodation for them. As one interviewee noted:

> [...] Another issue is, that we must see, is the vulnerable groups and all these special groups. Groups who came out either as cases of Gender-based violence, LGBTQI cases, [...] where there is no care. The only care that is been offered is only through the context of programmes of PRAKSIS, BABEL, EPAPSY, SOCIAL PSYCHIATRY, [...] and other

specific organisations, […] but they stop there. The system is not ready to neither support cases nor welcome cases that start from tracing to transferring, from providing to housing to all else. And I believe because we confront these [issues] on a daily basis, it's a basic part that must be in to all this that must be designed […] (Interviewee 1).

Participants in the focus group, argued that the shift from the emergency programmes of the past (NGOs funded by the EU) to the new ones (i.e., national integration programmes), revealed further the issues that surround the housing policy in Greece as there is "no appropriate transition" from the former to the latter. The latter had an immediate impact on the structures that used to house vulnerable groups such as unaccompanied minors, and these populations must be given priority. As one participant argued:

> […] if you cannot cover the local need, how can you cover the other? […] Many times the programmes you claim funding to cover actions doesn't allow you this, so there […] there must be again care at an institutional level. I don't know how this will happen, it requires a lot of discussion. But for example, […] I may be able to accommodate an LGBTQI case, refugee, with certain characteristics, after 2016, and receive care, and I may have a similar case where I have a Greek that I cannot accommodate. This itself introduces a bunch of issues, because the x programme binds me. […] So there is vicious cycle […] (Interviewee 1).

Other speakers during the focus group declared that there must be a stronger coordinated mechanism between the different stakeholders and a "central planning"[8] from the part of the state; while others argued that there are gaps in the current integration policy which fall under the general crisis that has affected the local population, *en masse,* on matters of health and social care, *vis-a-vis,* Greece. Furthermore, criticism was heard concerning the decision to withdraw NGOs from the camps such as the Red Cross, the Spanish Red Cross, Danish and the Greek Red Cross who took common

---

8 The word 'central planning' was heard many times during the focus group. Some participants argued there is no central planning, while others argued the opposite. Central planning was used many times abstractly, other times more concretely. In all cases it means that there must be stronger collaboration between the Ministry of Health and everybody else who works in the field of migration.

actions in the camps, but abandoned the field once the *PHILOS Programme* took over.

> The Red Cross, in collaboration with the Spanish Red Cross, Danish and Greek one, which were dealing with populations within structures, our departure occurred precisely because of the shift of EU policy [...] after the Philos programme took over [...] and we remained as Red Cross in the city of Athens and Attica Region, whereby we provide services of social and legal support, and psychological support [...] (Interviewee 6).

Both the literature review and the qualitative results of the focus group reveal important parameters in the domain of healthcare and social care that must be addressed. With regards to the current integration policy, and based on the focus group results, one could argue that at this stage one cannot talk of a concrete integration policy that is effectively implemented. Efforts are being made which at times are not well planned, neither well-coordinated. At the same time, participants argued that the policy does not encompass all migrants, but only those who are documented, and the discussion should include all Third Country Nationals who reside in the country. Moreover, even though there is wide acceptance of the sincere efforts being made at national level, still, those, remain "spasmodic" and "fragmented":

> [...] if there is no general, national plan, all of our efforts will be fragmented and spasmodic. If those [efforts] do not occur under the umbrella of the ministries, nothing will be done. We have seen this happening for many years. [...] I believe it is totally necessary to collaborate with everyone who has experience in this domain [...] (Interviewee 5).

Challenges and suggestions in this part of the chapter are drawn together as these crucial parameters summarize speakers' views as to the current integration policy. Some of these are: "better recording" of the problems at stake, active involvement of local communities, "central planning" from the part of the state, "stronger coordination" between the ministries and the NGOs in order to record the needs of those parts of the country that are not yet addressed, and a "unified plan" that will not only target migrants' needs, but the whole population. As one interviewee said:

> We need central planning, […] whenever and wherever is needed. Cause, I think no NGO can know all the needs of the whole country, whether it is the migrants, or vulnerable Greek population. If there is recording, […] and say, here there is a gap: come and do this […] then this is already a central planning […] (Interviewee 6).

The challenge still remains with respect to the accommodation needs of both Third Country Nationals and the destitute local population. It has been argued, that the duration of funding that covers accommodation needs, on the one hand binds NGOs to provide housing to specific groups of people within a strict time-line, on the other hand, it excludes other populations that face similar housing problems. On this matter one interviewee argued:

> […] we talk about a society which will welcome these people […] We don't want to divide these people, to Greeks and non-Greeks right? And at the same time one issue that results from all programmes is that all these programmes must consider the needs of the local population […] For example if the local population has analogous needs, that are not covered, those must be covered […] (Interviewee 2).

The latter coincides with the following suggestion; namely, to invigorate existing structures whereby TCNs reside and preserve their continuity, and increase the numbers of medical and paramedical personnel for the continuity of these actions. Having in mind all the above mentioned, one interviewee mentioned:

> We cannot talk about health, when we have this current model. You cannot take care of a person, if you don't and… I mention again …the accommodation issue for very specific reasons, because for there are unaccompanied minors who are not housed, and others who are about to leave [the accommodation scheme] shortly. Therefore, you cannot take care of a child if you don't have the rest […] (Interviewee 1).

Furthermore, it was stressed in the focus group that there must be an "intercultural efficiency" within hospitalisation, "task sharing" and "task-seeking" towards mental health, "decentralization", as well as an active participation of TCNs in trainings, having a leading role in the local communities. As far as the role of the municipalities is concerned, it has been suggested, that the former should be actively involved in the process of integration, as they have better knowledge of "the different needs" and "problems in each area". Regarding the contribution of the municipalities, it has been argued that:

> [...] There are many efforts from various municipalities, but the community and the involvement of the community along with the local stakeholders is very very important. For sure, it is important to have central planning, but I think, as time goes by, at local level, they will have a better say regarding management. Because, we should not forget that while we talk about the migrant/refugee issue, there are different needs, and different problems in each area, so it is important that there is involvement [...] (Interviewee7).

Again, with regards to healthcare, emphasis must be given towards education, training as to the importance of visiting a physician, awareness of cultural differences, and sensitising the public.

10. TOWARDS A CONCLUSION: SUGGESTIONS

Before closing this chapter, the reader should be informed as to the conditions under which the desk research took place. First, even though there is a variety of academic papers from 2010 onwards that address TCNs' needs in Greece, still there are many gaps regarding integration on matters of healthcare and social care at national level. Second, the absence of literature regarding integration reveals the lack of integration policy and vice versa. Third, the literature on best practices and the identification of those at empirical level derive mainly from the work of NGOs that highlight simultaneously the networks of collaboration and the latter are identified as best practices in the Greek scene, yet those practices not always have continuity, as maintaining an action for the integration of TCNs presupposes constant funding. And fourth, best practices in Greece relate more to the management of refugee crisis rather than integration, since migrant influx continues at national level.

In conclusion, this chapter has argued that there is no integration policy that is implemented in Greece regarding healthcare and social care. There was a brief remark as to the current situation of the country with reference to the financial crisis that still remains an obstacle in order to cover not just the needs of migrants but the whole population. Best practices have been also identified in the field of healthcare and social care at EU and national level, highlighting at the same time the indispensable work of NGOs in Greece that seek to fill in the gaps at national level, the networks of collaboration between state and non-state institutions, and the significance of intercultural mediation within public hospitals.

One could argue that more work needs to be done at national level on matters of healthcare and social care, informing third country nationals regarding their healthcare rights, identifying the needs of ultra-vulnerable groups such as unaccompanied minors, SGBV survivors and LGBTQI populations, and strengthening the housing policy in order for integration to render possible in the Greek society. To this end, the findings of the focus group can be also considered as a guiding force or else a formula for investigating a sustained model of integration as well as a tool for further research in Greece. It also informs the wider European community as to the constant assistance the country needs in order to integrate the new communities. The challenges and shortcomings in the field of healthcare and social care remain a concern in Greece and the findings of the focus group precipitate a chain of suggestions that may prove pivotal to bypass present barriers.

REFERENCES

Boussias, M. (2018). New health programme for refugees, *Health Daily*, 1505, 1-7 (in Greek).

Bradby, H., Humphris, R., Newall, D., and Phillimore, J. (2015). *Public health aspects of migrant health: a review of the evidence on health status for refugees and asylum seekers in the European Region.* Health Evidence Network Synthesis Report 44. Copenhagen: WHO Regional Office for Europe. Retrieved from: https://bit.ly/29ngdeU

European Web Site on Integration (EWSI). (2017a, August 3). Greece: Petition reporting on violation of asylum seekers' rights. Retrieved from: https://bit.ly/2YJp7xn

European Web Site on Integration (EWSI). (2017b, October 6). Equal access to vital maternal healthcare for vulnerable refugee women across Europe remains a challenge. Retrieved from: https://bit.ly/2Z xkQdH

Centre for Social Solidarity (EKKA). (2018). *Situation Update: Unaccompanied children (UAC) in Greece,* May 15, 2018. Athens: Centre for Social Solidarity (EKKA). Retrieved from: https://reliefwe b.int/sites/reliefweb.int/files/resources/63728.pdf

EN-HERA! (2009). *Sexual and reproductive health and rights of refugees, asylum seekers and undocumented migrants: A framework for the identification of good practices,* EN-HERA! Network, Belgium: Ghent. Retrieved from: https://bit.ly/33eOFC3

European Commission (2016). *Communication from the Commission to the European Parliament, the Council, the European Economic and Social Committee and the Committee of the Regions: Action Plan on the integration of third country nationals.* 7.6.2016 COM (2016) 377 final. Brussels: European Commission Retrieved from: https://bit.ly/ 2lqM7xB

European Migration Network (EMN). (2017). *2016 Annual Report on Migration and Asylum.* Brussels: European Migration Network (EMN) Retrieved from: https://bit.ly/2qZE3CX

European Commission. (2018). *Special Eurobarometer 469: Report: Integration of Immigrants in the European Union.* Brussels: Directorate-General for Migration and Home Affairs/European Union. doi: 10.2837/918822

Chiarenza, A., Abraham, E., Atungo, S., Coune, I., Fortier, J.P., Ramirez, M.G., …. Verrept, H. (2014). *Standards for equity in health care for migrants and other vulnerable groups.* Task Force on Migrant-Friendly and Culturally Competent Health Care Regional HPH Network of Emilia-Romagna. DOI: 10.13140/RG.2.2.27349.93928

Gkionakis, N. (2016). The Refugee crisis in Greece: Training border security, police, volunteers and aid workers in psychological first aid, *Intervention, 14*(1), 73-79. Retrieved from: https://bit.ly/2TdbdhZ

Hatzopoulos, V., Fouskas, T., Grigoriou, P., Karabelias, G., Kazanas, K., Mine, F., de Maio, A., Novak, C., and Pechlidi, G. (2018). *European Migration Network: Annual Report 2017 on Migration and Asylum in Greece: National Report: Part 2. European Migration Network.* Athens: European Public Law Organization (EPLO)/Hellenic Ministry for Migration Policy/European Commission/European Migration Network (EMN). Retrieved from: https://bit.ly/2M3W2GW

CARE (2017). *Health tracking and monitoring system: User manual.* (no.01, 13/01/2017) report under the Common approach for refugees and other migrants' health (CARE) project, funded by the European Union's Health Programme (2014-2020). Retrieved from: https://bit.ly/2KuKNEr

International Organization for Migration (IOM). (2016). *Summary Report on the MIPEX health strand and country reports.* IOM Migration Research Series, 52. Geneva: International Organization for Migration (IOM). Retrieved from: https://bit.ly/2kmwR3G

International Organization for Migration (IOM). (2017). *Migration legal guide for practitioners in Greece.* Athens: International Organization for Migration (IOM) Retrieved from: https://bit.ly/2OF3wlT

International Organization for Migration (IOM). (2019). *Glossary on Migration.* International Migration Law. no.4. Geneva: International Organization for Migration (IOM) Retrieved from: https://bit.ly/2RFilTq

Karavaltsiou, V. (2017, June 20). The Refugee Children became Adults in Greece. And Now? *CNN Greece.* Retrieved from: https://bit.ly/2YQxXJK (in Greek)

Marouda, M., Saranti, V., Koutsouraki, E. & Kakkalou, E. (2014). *Access of Migrants in Social Security and Sanitary Care: Policies and Practice in Greece.* Athens: Institute of International Relations/Ministry of Interior/European Commission/European Migration Network (EMN). Retrieved from: https://bit.ly/31nVJdP

Mikaba, P. (2018). *Migrant health across Europe: Little structural policies, many encouraging practices.* Retrieved from: https://bit.ly/2 Tks0Qp.

Ministry for Migration Policy/Asylum Service. (2018a). *Statistical data of the Asylum Service-AIDA REPORT ON GREECE 2017.* Athens: Ministry for Migration Policy/Asylum Service. Retrieved from: https://bit.ly/2FBeDGW (in Greek)

Ministry for Migration Policy/Asylum Service. (2018b). *Asylum procedures* from 07.06.2013 to 30.06.2018. Athens: Ministry for Migration Policy/Asylum Service. Retrieved from: https://bit.ly/2vDti LA.

Ministry for Migration Policy/Asylum Service (2018c). *Statistical Data of the Greek Asylum Service* from 7.06.2013 to 30.06.2018. Athens: Ministry for Migration Policy/Asylum Service. Retrieved from: https://bit.ly/2vyPhDu

Mladovsky, P., Ingleby, D., McKee, M., & Rechel., B. (2012). Good practices in migrant health: the European experience. *Clinical Medicine,12*(3), 248-252. Retrieved from: https://bit.ly/33iYheX

National Health Operations Centre (EKEPY). (2017a). *Health Working Group Meeting*, 22/03/2017. Press Release. Athens: National Health Operations Centre (EKEPY). Retrieved from: https://bit.ly/2OJFUwB (in Greek)

Papadaki, M., Lionis, C., Saridaki, A., Dowrick, C., de Brún, T., O'Reilly-de Brún, M., O'Donnell, C., Burns. N., van Weel-Baumgarten, E., van den Muijsenbergh, M., Spiegel, W., & MacFarlane, A. (2017). Exploring barriers to primary care for migrants in Greece in times of austerity: Perspectives of service providers. *European Journal of General Practice*, *23*(1), 128-134, doi:10.1080/13814788.2017.130 7336

Portugal, R., Padilla, B., Ingleby, D., de Freitas, C., Lebas, J. & Pereira Miguel, J. (eds.) (2007). *Good practices on health and migration in the EU: Health and Migration in the EU: Better health for all in an inclusive society.* Lisbon: Ministerio da Saude/Saude e Migracoes na UE. Retrieved from: https://bit.ly/2yHZVZO

Psoinos, M., Karamanidou, C., Albiani, S., Tizzi, G., Borgioli, G., Pinilla José Caldés, M., Pezzati, P., Ioannidis, E., Papamichail, D., & Koulierakis, G. (2016). *Good practices report about civil society organisations and their role on health assessment and preventive measures.* CARE: Deliverable D8.2 (WP8) report under the Common approach for refugees and other migrants' health (CARE) project, funded by the European Union's Health Programme (2014-2020).

Safe Passage UK & PRAKSIS (2017, March 17). UK Home Office publishes criteria for 'Dubs scheme' refugee children from Greece, leaving the majority ineligible. Press Release. Retrieved from: https://bit.ly/2GDZXpW (in Greek)

Seedat, F., Hargreaves, S., Nellums, L., Ouyang, J., Brown, M., & Friedland, J. (2018). How effective are approaches to migrant screening for infectious diseases in Europe? A Systematic review. *Lancet Infectious Diseases, 18*(9), 259-271. doi: 10.1016/S1473-3099 (18)30117-8

Skleparis, D. (2018). *Refugee Integration in Mainland Greece: Prospects and Challenges.* Policy Brief 02, March 2018, Ismir: Yasar University UNESCO Chair on International Migration. Retrieved from: https://bit.ly/2YLYvb9

Sparrow, A. (2017, December 22). Efforts to resettle child refugees under Dubs scheme 'completely inadequate'. *The Guardian.* Retrieved from: https://bit.ly/30wehJl

Taylor, D. (2017, December 15). First vulnerable refugee child arrives in UK from Greece under Dubs scheme. *The Guardian.* Retrieved from: https://bit.ly/2Bv72HR

Home Office. (2016). *Policy Statement: Section 67 of the Immigration Act 2016, Updated December 2018.* ('The Dubs Amendment'). United Kingdom: Home Office. Retrieved from: https://bit.ly/2SRhL4X

UN General Assembly. (1966). *International Covenant on Economic, Social and Cultural Rights.* 16 December 1966. United Nations, Treaty Series, vol. 993. New York: UN General Assembly. Retrieved from: http://www.refworld.org/docid/3ae6b36c0.html

United Nations High Commissioner for Refugees (UNHCR). (2018a, May 28). Europe Monthly Report: April 2018. Retrieved from: https://bit.ly/2KtSxGT

United Nations High Commissioner for Refugees (UNHCR). (2018b, May 30). Weekly Accommodation Update. Retrieved from: https://bit.ly/2YL9rd8

World Health Organization (WHO). (2015). Greece: assessing health-system capacity to manage large influxes of migrants: Joint report on a mission of the Ministry of Health of Greece, Hellenic Center for Disease Control and Prevention and WHO Regional Office for Europe. Copenhagen: WHO Regional Office for Europe. Retrieved from: https://bit.ly/2LSMIl4

World Health Organization (WHO). (2016, January 25). WHO/Europe open new page in collaboration with the Greek Ministry of Health. Retrieved from: https://bit.ly/2YstttJ

World Health Organization (WHO). (2018). *Report on the health of refugees and migrants in the WHO European Region: No PUBLIC HEALTH without REFUGEE and MIGRANT HEALTH.* Copenhagen: WHO Regional Office for Europe. Retrieved from: https://bit.ly/2VctgoN

Reviewed by: Gerassimos Karabelias, Professor, Department of Sociology, Panteion University of Social and Political Sciences, Greece.

In: Advances in Sociology Research   ISBN: 978-1-53616-781-8
Editor: Jared A. Jaworski   © 2020 Nova Science Publishers, Inc.

Chapter 3

CYBERBULLYING THROUGH SOCIAL NETWORKING WEBSITES

Michelle F. Wright
Penn State University and Masaryk University

ABSTRACT

The purpose of this chapter is to examine cyberbullying through social media among youth. An extension of traditional bullying, cyberbullying is a form of bullying which takes place by means of electronic technologies, such as email, instant messaging, social media, and text messaging through mobile devices. Drawing on research from a variety of disciplines, such as psychology, education, social work, sociology, and computer science, this chapter is organized into six sections. These sections include: (1) explaining the definitions, technologies used, the role of anonymity, and prevalence rates of cyberbullying, (2) discussing the characteristics and risk factors associated with cyberbullying involvement, (3) reviewing research findings on the psychosocial and behavioral consequences resulting from cyberbullying involvement, (4) discussing strategies to prevent cyberbullying and recommendations, (5) explaining future research directions, and (6) closing remarks about cyberbullying. The chapter draws on multidisciplinary qualitative, quantitative, and mixed-design research methodologies.

Youths have fully embraced digital technologies, with many of them using social networking websites daily (Lenhart, 2015). Digital technologies enable various opportunities for youths, including rapid communication at almost any time of the day, acquisition of knowledge for leisure and homework, and entertainment. There is also a darker side to youths' interactions with digital media, including their exposure to negative online situations through social networking websites. They might be exposed to unwanted, gory, and sexually explicit graphic content through videos, images, and text. Online problematic situations might also involve identity theft and sexual predation. Cyberbullying is another negative consequence associated with youths' use of social networking websites.

Cyberbullying is defined as being targeted with negative behaviors through digital technologies, specifically through email, instant messaging, social networking websites, and text messages through mobile phones (Bauman, Underwood, & Card, 2013; Grigg, 2012). The cyber context allows cyberbullies to mask or hide their identity while interacting in cyberspace. Because cyberbullies can be anonymous online, they are afforded greater flexibility when harming their victims and they can do so without witnessing the negative reactions of the victims and/or experiencing any negative consequences associated with their actions (Wright, 2014b). Anonymity can trigger the online disinhibition effect in which youths might do or say something to others online that they would never do or say offline (Suler, 2004; Wright, 2014a). Rapid transmission of communication is another component of digital technologies which allows cyberbullies to target their victims in a much quicker and expansive context. An offline rumor might take many hours, even days, to spread around school, while such a rumor might take seconds to spread in the online world. It is also possible to target victims as often as cyberbullies want as it is tough to escape bullying in the online world, as digital technology access is available almost anywhere. The number of potential bystanders increases in the cyber context, wherein these individuals can continue the cycle of cyberbullying through sharing of content with others.

The purpose of this chapter is to review literature on cyberbullying through social networking websites among youths in elementary, middle, and high school. The research reviewed incorporates studies from different disciplines, including psychology, education, communication, social work, sociology, media studies, computer science and information technology, and gender studies. The studies also involve cross-sectional, longitudinal, qualitative, quantitative, and mixed-methods research designs. There are seven sections included in this literature review:

(a) Introduction to Cyberbullying – provides definition of cyberbullying, characteristics of cyberbullying, and the prevalence rates of cyberbullying in the United States.

(b) Risk Factors for Cyberbullying – reviews risk factors associated with youths' involvement in cyberbullying.

(c) Psychosocial and Academic Consequences of Cyberbullying – describes research findings concerning the psychological, social, behavioral, and academic consequences of youths' cyberbullying involvement.

(d) Strategies and Recommendations – explains suggestions for prevention and intervention programs designed to reduce cyberbullying involvement.

(e) Future Research Directions – discussion of various recommendations for research aimed at understanding more about youths' involvement in cyberbullying.

(f) Conclusion – focuses on closing remarks regarding the nature of the literature on youths' cyberbullying.

INTRODUCTION TO CYBERBULLYING

Defined as youths' use of digital technologies to harass, embarrass, and intimidate others with hostile intent, cyberbullying can involve an imbalance of power between the perpetrator and the victim and include repetition, similar the definition of traditional face-to-face bullying (Smith et al., 2013). Cyberbullying might involve cyberbullies targeting a victim once or multiple times by sharing a humiliating and embarrassing video, picture, or text message to one person or many people (Bauman et al., 2013). Repetition is further important as applied to negative online behaviors because sending a video, picture, or a text message to even one person could trigger that particular person to share the content another with one other person or multiple people, who could then share that content again with a new person or people. The cyclic nature of cyberbullying is complex because of the potential repetitiveness of cyberbullying behaviors.

Perpetrating and experiencing negative behaviors through digital technologies is another component of the cyberbullying definition which separates it from the definition of traditional face-to-face bullying (Curelaru, Iacob, & Abalasi, 2009). Various technologies can be used to perpetrate cyberbullying behaviors, such as social networking websites, text messages through mobile devices, chat programs, and online gaming. The most frequently utilized technologies to harm others include gaming consoles, instant messaging tools, and social networking websites (Ybarra et al., 2007). Cyberbullying behaviors include distributing unkind, mean, and/or hateful content through text messages, chat programs, and emails, as well as identity theft, pretending to be someone else, sharing secrets about a victim, spreading nasty rumors through social networking websites, threats of harm in the offline world, and uploading pictures or videos of someone who does not want it shared (Bauman et al., 2013). Oftentimes cyberbullying behaviors are similar to those in the offline world, including experiencing/perpetrating harassment, insults, verbal attacks, teasing, physical threats, social exclusion, gossip, and humiliation.

There are some cyberbullying behaviors without a face-to-face equivalent. Cyberbullies can create defamatory websites and social networking profiles (Rideout et al., 20015). Happy slapping is another form of cyberbullying behavior. It involves a group of people who randomly assault someone while the incident is being filmed by a mobile phone and is then posted online for others to view/watch. Another type of cyberbullying behavior is flaming. Flaming involves posting a provocative/offensive message in a public forum/discussion with the intent of provoking a hostile response or triggering an argument with other individuals.

Prevalence Rates of Cyberbullying

Most of the earliest research on cyberbullying focused on the prevalence rates of perpetration, victimization, and bystanding. Kowalski and Limber (2007) found that 11% of the 3,767 middle school students (aged 11-14) in their sample were cyberbullied at least once, 4% had bullied others, and 7% were involved as perpetrators and victims combined. Slightly higher rates were found by Patchin and Hinduja (2006). In their study, Patchin and Hinduja found that 29% of youths in their sample were cybervictims and 47% were bystanders of cyberbullying. In another study, with an older sample of youths (grades 9th through 12th), Goebert et al. (2011) found that 56.1% of their sample from Hawaii reported that they were cybervictims. These studies focused on younger age groups of youths, although cyberbullying usually is highest among early adolescents, encompassing youths in middle school and high school. Therefore, in a follow-up study, Hinduja and Patchin (2012) examined cyberbullying experiences of youths in grades 6th through 12th. Of their sample, 4.9% indicated that they were cyberbullies in the past 30 days. Variations in prevalence rates are attributed to differences in sampling and measurement techniques. Despite such differences, the rates of cyberbullying among youths indicate that this behavior is a concern worthy of attention.

RISK FACTORS FOR CYBERBULLYING

Although the research on prevalence rates of cyberbullying revealed differences in rates based on sample and measurement, it increases researchers concern with cyberbullying, leading them to focus on the risk factors associated with cyberbullying. In one of the earliest studies on risk factors of cyberbullying, Williams and Guerra (2007) focused on the association between age and these behaviors. They found that cyberbullying victimization was highest in early adolescence than in late adolescence, while perpetration of cyberbullying was highest in late adolescence. Physical forms of cyberbullying (e.g., hacking) peaked in middle school and then declined during high school. Another study revealed that cyberbullying involvement was highest among 9th graders when compared to middle school students (Wade & Beran, 2011), indicating that age might not be the best predictor of cyberbullying, due to inconsistent findings in the literature.

Gender has also been examined in relation to cyberbullying involvement among youths. This research has revealed that boys were more often the perpetrators of cyberbullying when compared to girls (Boulton et al., 2012; Li, 2007; Ybarra et al., 2007), while other researchers (e.g., Dehue, Bolman, &Vollink, 2008; Pornari & Wood, 2010) concluded that girls were more often cyberbullies in comparison to boys. Studies by Hinduja and Patchin (2007) and Kowalski and Limber (2007) suggested that girls reported more cyberbullying victimization than boys, whereas Huang and Chou (2010) and Sjurso et al. (2016) found that boys were more often cybervictims. Other researchers have found no effect of gender when predicting youths' cyberbullying involvement (e.g., Stoll & Block, 2015; Wright & Li, 2013b). Therefore, gender might not be the best predictor of cyberbullying involvement.

Attention has also been given to the role of youths' offline experiences with traditional face-to-face bullying in their cyberbullying involvement. Findings from these studies revealed that cyberbullying perpetration and traditional face-to-face bullying perpetration, cyberbullying victimization and traditional face-to-face victimization, and cyberbullying perpetration and traditional face-to-face victimization are positively related (Barlett & Gentile, 2012; Mitchell et al., 2007; Wright & Li, 2013a; Wright & Li, 2013b).

Digital technology use is also a risk factor associated with youths' cyberbullying involvement. The conclusion from this research is that digital technology use increases youths' risk of cyberbullying perpetration and victimization. Ang (2016) and Aricak et al. (2008) found that high internet use was related positively to cyberbullying involvement among youths. In addition, Smith and colleagues (2008) found that cybervictims spent more time using instant messaging tools, email, blogging sites, and online games than nonvictims. To explain the relationship between digital technology use and cyberbullying involvement, Ybarra et al. (2007) explained that youths who spent more time online are much more likely to disclose personal information online, such as their geographic location. Such self-disclosures increase youths' risk of cyberbullying victimization.

Externalizing problems (e.g., alcohol use) and internalizing problems (e.g., depression, loneliness) are related positively to youths' involvement in cyberbullying (Cappadocia et al., 2013; Wright, in press). These associations might be explained by cybervictims having an inability or reduced ability to cope with victimization, which increases their vulnerability to cyberbullying victimization (Cappadocia et al., 2013; Mitchell et al., 2007).

Other characteristics and personal characteristics are associated with youths' cyberbullying involvement. Normative beliefs (i.e., belief that aggression is an acceptable form of behavior) are related positively to face-to-face bullying and cyberbullying perpetration (e.g., Burton, Florell, &Wygant, 2013; Wright, 2014b). Oftentimes cyberbullies perceive cyberbullying as an acceptable behavior and as an acceptable response for a perceived injustice. Provictim attitudes (i.e., belief that bullying is unacceptable and that defending victims is valuable and necessary) also relate to cyberbullying involvement. In particular, lower provictim attitudes increases cyberbullying perpetration (Sevcikova, Machackova, Wright, Dedkova, &Cerna, 2015). Other variables, including low peer attachment, less self-control, less empathetic concern, and greater moral disengagement were related positively to cyberbullying perpetration (Wright, Kamble, Lei, Li, Aoyama, & Shruti, 2015).

Most of the research on the personal characteristics associated with cyberbullying involvement incorporate cross-sectional research designs. Such a limitation of the literature reduces our ability to understand the long-term associations of these characteristics and risk factors associated with cyberbullying involvement. In one of the few longitudinal studies, Fanti et al. (2012) found that youths' exposure to violent media content and their endorsement of high callous and unemotional traits increased their cyberbullying perpetration one year later. In addition, greater exposure to media violence exposure increased the risk of cyberbullying victimization. Perceived levels of stress from parents, peers, and academics also have a role in adolescents' perpetration of cyberbullying one year later (Wright, 2014a).

The research reviewed in this section suggests that there are various characteristics and risk factors associated with youths' involvement in cyberbullying. This section involved discussing research which focused on individual or personal characteristics and cyberbullying. Available research also suggests that there are other contextual predictors, including parents, schools, and teachers, have a role in youths' cyberbullying involvement.

Parents as Risk Factors

Ample research has revealed that parenting styles are associated with youths' cyberbullying perpetration and victimization. Totura et al. (2009) found that youths who were identified as bully-victims often reported that their parents utilized indifferent-uninvolved parenting styles and inconsistent monitoring of their activities were related to cyberbullying perpetration and victimization. Neglectful parenting, also known as indifferent-uninvolved parenting, increased youths' involvement in cyberbullying when compared to uninvolved youths (Dehue, Bolman, Vollink, & Pouwelse, 2012).

Indifferent-uninvolved parents are often emotionally distant from their children, engage in little or no supervision, show little warmth and affection toward their children, place fewer demands on their children's behaviors, and intentionally avoid their children. Cyber victimization was also increased among children who reported that their parents engaged in authoritarian parenting styles (Dehue et al., 2012). Authoritarian parenting style is defined as parents who have high levels of demands and low levels of responsiveness. These parents have very high expectation but they display very low levels of warmth or nurturance toward their children.

Parental monitoring is another aspect of parenting receiving attention in the online environment. Approximately 50% of children in one study reported that their parents monitored their online activities (Mason, 2008). Another study found that children and their parents differed in their report of parental monitoring. In this study, McQuade et al. (2009) found that 93% of parents reported that they engaged in some type of parenting monitoring activity/strategy. However, 37% of their children reported that their parents had rules regarding their online activities. The discrepancy between children's and parents' reports might be due to parents overestimating the amount of monitoring they engage in. It could also mean that parents implement ineffective strategies. Additional attention should be given to how parents navigate conversations with their children about online risks and opportunities.

Some researchers have considered parental monitoring and parental mediation as strategies that can help reduce youths' exposure to negative online experiences, such as cyberbullying. In one study on this topic, Wright (2015) found that high levels of parental mediation of youths' technology use reduced the negative adjustment difficulties resulting from experiencing high levels of cyber victimization. Wright explained that parental monitoring encourages discussion of the risk associated with cyberbullying involvement, which might mitigate or reduce the likelihood of being exposed further to cyberbullying. During such discussions, parents might make it clear that cyberbullying is unacceptable, as well as provide social support and other strategies to reduce cyberbullying risk. Such a proposal is supported by the literature as Hinduja and Patchin (2013) and Wright (2013a) found that youths who were concerned with being punished for negative online behaviors were much less likely to perpetrate cyberbullying. However, Aoyama and colleagues (2011) did not find support for parental monitoring preventing youths' cyberbullying involvement. They found that parental monitoring and mediation were unrelated to cyberbullying perpetration and victimization. To explain these findings, Aoyama et al. mentioned that parents lack technological skills to effectively monitor their children's online activities. This makes it difficult for parents to know when and how to intervene in these activities. It might also be likely that parents attempt to implement rules but do not follow-up on what they implement. Not further discussing or implementing these rules could give the impression to youths that their parents are not concerned with appropriate online behaviors, potentially increasing the risk of cyberbullying involvement. Failing to enforce rules might also indicate that parents do not often update strategies as their children become more independent electronic technology users. Rosen (2007) found that parents report that they are often unsure how to discuss online activities with their children. Being unsure about what to say or discuss might decrease the likelihood that parents discuss appropriate online behavior with their children. However, more research is needed as many parents nowadays are just as connected to their devices and many understand how to navigate digital technologies.

Research has also been conducted on other family characteristics and how such characteristics influence youths' involvement in cyberbullying. In particular, Ybarra and Mitchell (2004) found that family income, parental education, and marital status of caregivers were unrelated to cyberbullying perpetration or victimization. Some research has found that parental unemployment was related positively to cyberbullying involvement (Arslan, Savaser, Hallett, & Balci, 2012). This section considered family, parent-child relationships, and parental monitoring and mediation in youths' cyberbullying involvement. Another factor investigated in the literature is the role of school, which is discussed next.

Schools as Risk Factors

The role of schools in monitoring and punishing youths' involvement in cyberbullying is complicated and is a topic of great debate among schools, parents, authorities, and researchers. Many incidences of cyberbullying occur off school grounds, making it difficult for schools to be aware of such incidences (deLara, 2012; Mason, 2008).

However, many of these incidences involve youths who attend the same school, increasing the complexity of the schools' role in handling situations of cyberbullying. Given that there is a high likelihood that cyberbullies and cybervictims are from the same school, it is possible that information/knowledge about the cyberbullying situation could spread throughout the school. This could lead to further negative interactions between youths while on school grounds, which could disrupt the learning process.

Even when cyberbullying incidences "spill over" onto school grounds", administrations, teachers, and school districts have vastly different perceptions and awareness of these situations. It is likely that some individuals in the school environment might not perceive cyberbullying as a significant event, warranting attention and consequences (Kochenderfer-Ladd & Pelletier, 2008). Some administrators and teachers do not perceive covert forms of bullying, like relational bullying and cyberbullying, as serious and harmful, making it difficult for them to understand the consequences of these types of bullying (Sahin, 2010). They are quick to consider physical bullying as problematic. Not viewing cyberbullying as problematic is an issue especially considering that digital technologies are embedded almost completely or even completely in youths' lives. When administrators, staff, and teachers do not perceive cyberbullying as problematic, they are unlikely to help youths who experiences these behaviors by helping them cope or deal with the situation. Instead, administrators, staff, and teachers might minimize the experience.

There is also evidence that teacher training does not properly inform teachers on how to deal with and recognize cyberbullying. Such limitations of teacher training make it difficult for teachers to intervene in cyberbullying incidences. In one study, Cassidy and colleagues (2012a) found that many Canadian teachers reported that they were unfamiliar with newer technologies. Not knowing about or understanding digital technologies prevents teachers from dealing effectively with cyberbullying as they are often unsure about how to respond to such incidences or how to implement strategies to address the situation. Even when teachers are concerned with cyberbullying, their school district may lack policies and programs to deal with these experiences (Cassidy, Brown, &Jackson, 2012b). This makes it difficult for teachers to implement solutions and strategies to deal with cyberbullying.

Tangen and Campbell (2010) found that teachers were more willing to participate in prevention and intervention programs focused on traditional face-to-face bullying than they were interested in participating in cyberbullying prevention and intervention programs. This finding might reflect limitations of such programs as there are few empirically and theoretically grounded cyberbullying prevention or intervention programs. A more alarming explanation for Tangen and Campbell's (2010) finding is that some teachers do not consider cyberbullying an important issue to warrant attention. Recognizing the importance of implementing policies and training programs on cyberbullying is important because youths' involvement in these behaviors has the potential to impact the learning environment (Shariff & Hoff, 2007).

Teacher training is greatly needed to increase their awareness of cyberbullying. Such training might make it possible for teachers to help develop policies at the school level to reduce and punish cyberbullying. It is also important that teachers increase their confidence with dealing with cyberbullying as a means to increase their commitment to their school and increase their desire to learn more about cyberbullying (Eden et al., 2013). A greater awareness of cyberbullying can help teachers deal effectively with it to help prevent youths' involvement in these behaviors (Elledge et al., 2013). Teachers' motivation for learning about cyberbullying decreases from elementary school to middle school (Ybarra et al., 2007). Such a finding is problematic as cyberbullying increases from the elementary school years to the middle school years. Thus, there is a strong need for educator training programs aimed at raising awareness of cyberbullying, particularly in the middle school years.

Perpetrators and victims of cyberbullying are less likely to perceive their school and teachers positively when compared to uninvolved youths (Bayar & Ucanok, 2012). Because cyberbullying can involve peers from youths' schools, they might fear that a cyberbully could be a classmate.

Being fearful of cyberbullies can decrease youths' concentration on learning, reducing their academic persistence, attainment, and performance (Eden, Heiman, & Olenik-Shemesh, 2013). Lower school commitment and perceptions of a negative school climate increase children's and adolescents' engagement in cyberbullying as they feel less connected to their school (Williams & Guerra, 2007). Youths' involvement in cyberbullying is linked to poor academic functioning (Wright, 2015).

Youths' peers are present in both the offline and online world. Through peer interactions, youths learn about social norms and standards. Such social norms and standards dictate acceptable and unacceptable behaviors within the peer group, even if the behaviors are negative. Supporting this proposal, Festl and colleagues (2013) found that the highest levels of cyberbullying involvement occur in classrooms in which these behaviors are elevated. This finding may suggest that school climate might increase cyberbullying behaviors within a particular classroom. Believing that one's friends also engage in cyberbullying increases youths' risk of cyberbullying perpetration (Hinduja & Patchin, 2013). Peer contagion might explain the associations between youths' friends engaging in cyberbullying and one's cyberbullying perpetration, suggesting that one's friends "spread" negative online behaviors to others within their social network (Sijtsema, Ashwin, Simona, & Gina, 2014).

Peer attachment (i.e., closeness that youths feel with their same or similarly aged peers) is another peer-related variable related to cyberbullying involvement. Low peer attachment was related positively to cyberbullying involvement (Burton et al., 2013). Believing that one's peers will not be there for them when they are needed is characteristic of low peer attachment, which promotes negative interactions with peers. Research has revealed that cyberbullying is greater for youths who experience peer rejection (Sevcikova et al., 2015; Wright & Li, 2013b). Wright and Li (2012) argue that peer rejection triggers negative emotional responses that leads to cyberbullying perpetration and victimization.

Another body of literature suggests that cyberbullying perpetration might be motivated by youths' desire to maintain and boost their social standing in their peer group. Wright (2014c) found that perceived popularity (a reputational type of popularity in the peer group) was related to cyberbullying perpetration six months later, after controlling for previous levels of cyberbullying perpetration. Given the increased rates of cyberbullying in the middle school years and that the desire for popularity increases during these years as well, Wright proposes that digital technologies might be utilized as tools for the promotion and maintenance of their social standing.

PSYCHOSOCIAL AND ACADEMIC OUTCOMES OF YOUTH'S CYBERBULLYING

It was not only the frequency rates of cyberbullying that triggered concerns with cyberbullying, but also the psychosocial and academic outcomes associated with this experience. The linkages between psychosocial and academics outcomes and cyberbullying is attributed to this experience disrupting youths' emotional experiences, increasing their vulnerability to negative outcomes, because of negative coping strategies. When compared to nonvictims, cybervictims report lower global happiness, school happiness, school satisfaction, family satisfaction, and self-satisfaction (Toledano, Werch, & Wiens, 2015). Furthermore, cybervictims have greater feelings of anger, sadness, and fear than noninvolved youths (Dehue et al., 2008; Machackova, Dedkova, Sevcikova, & Cerna, 2013; Patchin & Hinduja, 2006).

Cyberbullying perpetration and victimization are linked to youths' poor academic performance. Youths involved in cyberbullying have an increased risk for difficulties at school, including academic problems, less motivation for school, poor academic performance, lower academic attainment, and more school absences (Belae & Hall, 2007; Yousef & Bellamy, 2015). Many of these studies involve self-reports of academic-related outcomes. Using school records, Wright (2015) also found that cyberbullying perpetration and victimization is linked to lower school functioning.

Researchers (e.g., Mitchell, Ybarra, & Finkelhor, 2007; Patchin & Hinduja, 2006; Wright, 2014b; Ybarra, Diener-West, & Leaf, 2007) have also found that youths' internalizing and externalizing difficulties are also associated with their involvement in cyberbullying. In the literature, cyberbullies and cybervictims report experiencing suicidal thoughts and attempt suicide more often than uninvolved youths (Bauman, Toomey, & Walker 2013). Beckman et al. (2012) also found similar results as Bauman et al. (2013). In particular, they found that cyberbullying involvement increased the risk of youths experiencing mental health problems. Expanding on these findings, Sourander et al. (2012) found that these youths are also at risk for psychiatric and psychosomatic problems (Sourander et al., 2010).

The literature on the psychosocial and academic consequences of cyberbullying are limited because many times researchers do not account for youths' involvement in traditional face-to-face bullying. Such a focus is important as youths involved in cyberbullying perpetration and/or victimization are often victims and/or bullies of traditional face-to-face bullying (Williams & Guerra, 2007; Wright & Li, 2013b). Bonanno and colleagues (2013) accounted for traditional face-to-face bullying involvement in their study by including it into their model. They found that the psychosocial consequences of cyberbullying perpetration and victimization was greater when compared to face-to-face bullying perpetration and victimization.

Because of the positive correlation between youths' involvement in cyberbullying and traditional face-to-face bullying, some researchers have investigated the combined impacts of these experiences on youths' psychosocial and academic consequences. Gradinger et al. (2009) and Perren et al. (2012) found that victims of both types of bullying reported greater internalizing difficulties than youths who experienced only one type of victimization.

In sum, the research has revealed that experiencing both face-to-face bullying and cyberbullying exacerbates youths' psychosocial and academic consequences. Such research suggests the importance of considering youths' involvement in various bullying behaviors. Understanding the impact of cyberbullying is important as it can provide details about the best ways to intervene.

SOLUTIONS AND RECOMMENDATIONS

Cyberbullying should be considered a public health concern. It requires attention from all members of society. Education curriculum should include digital literacy skills training and citizenship in both the online and offline worlds (Cassidy et al., 2012b). This curriculum should present a balance view of digital technologies, including also providing details about the positive use of such technologies, as well as provide information to youths on empathy building, self-esteem, and social skills. School climate should also be improved by having teachers, school administration, and staff learn students' names, praise good behavior both online and offline, and become and stay technologically informed and up-to-date (Hinduja & Patchin, 2012).

Schools and parents should not attempt to tackle cyberbullying independently. They should partner to help address cyberbullying together. It is important that parents identify their gaps in digital technology knowledge and increase their awareness of what their children do online (Cassidy et al., 2012a; Diamanduros & Downs, 2011). Increasing one's knowledge impacts parents' understanding of how to recognize the risks and opportunities associated with digital technologies. It can help parents implement more effective monitoring strategies when they have more knowledge about digital technologies and cyberbullying. Parents must maintain and engage in an open dialogue with their children about digital technologies use.

FUTURE RESEARCH DIRECTIONS

Although this chapter provides a comprehensive review of cyberbullying involvement among youths, there are some noticeable gaps in the literature which can be addressed by research. Cyberbullying is often hypothesized to be perpetrated due to the anonymity offered by digital technologies. Despite such a proposal, little attention has been given to this topic. Future research should focus on the youths' perceptions of anonymous acts online and the factors which might motivate youths to engage in cyberbullying research. It is also important to understand whether coping strategies might differ for anonymous versus non-anonymous cyberbullying, and whether adjustment difficulties are more pronounced with one type of cyberbullying than the other. There are few longitudinal studies on youths' cyberbullying involvement, which warrants additional research. Intervention and prevention programs could be developed which specific consideration to the specific age group identified as at the most risk for cyberbullying involvement.

CONCLUSION

The premise of this chapter was to provide a review of the literature on youths' involvement in cyberbullying, as well as provide next directions for intervention, prevention, public policy, and research. Despite a firm foundation for understand youth's cyberbullying prevalence, risks, and outcomes, there are still some gaps in the literature. Much of the older research on cyberbullying focused on the prevalence rates of youths' involvement, with research shifting to more currently focus on the predictors, causes, and consequences of youths' cyberbullying involvement. Research is still in its early stages concerning the comparison of both traditional face-to-face bullying and cyberbullying. Future research should also aim to understand more about the contextual predictors of cyberbullying, including the role of parents, schools, peers, and communities. Cyberbullying should be considered a negative behavior which impacts many levels of our society and undermines ethical and moral values.

REFERENCES

Ang, R. P. (2016). Cyberbullying: Its prevention and intervention strategies. In D. Sibnath (Ed.), *Child safety, welfare and well-being: Issues and challenges,* (pp. 25-38). New, NY: Springer.

Aoyama, I., Utsumi, S. & Hasegawa, M. (2011). Cyberbullying in Japan: Cases, government reports, adolescent relational aggression and parental monitoring roles. In Q. Li, D. Cross, & P. K. Smith (Eds.), *Bullying in the global playground: Research from an international perspective. Oxford, UK: Wiley-Blackwell.*

Aricak, T., Siyahhan, S., Uzunhasanoglu, A., Saribeyoglu, S., Ciplak, S., Yilmaz, N. & Memmedov, C. (2008). Cyberbullying among Turkish adolescents. *Cyber Psychology & Behavior, 11, 253-261.*

Arslan, S., Savaser, S., Hallett, V. & Balci, S. (2012). Cyberbullying among primary school students in Turkey: Self-reported prevalence and associations with home and school life. *Cyber Psychology, Behavior, and Social Networking, 15, 527-533.*

Ayas, T. & Horzum, M. B. (2010). Cyberbullg/victim scale development study. Retrieved from: http://www.akademikbakis.org.

Barlett, C. P. & Gentile, D. A. (2012). Long-term psychological predictors of cyber-bullying in late adolescence. *Psychology of Popular Media Culture, 2,* 123-135.

Barlett, C. P., Gentile, D. A., Anderson, C. A., Suzuki, K., Sakamoto, A., Yamaoka, A. & Katsura, R. (2013). Cross-cultural differences in cyberbullying behavior: A short-term longitudinal study. *Journal of Cross-Cultural Psychology, 45,* 300-313.

Bauman, S., Toomey, R. B. & Walker, J. L. (2013). Associations among bullying, cyberbullying, and suicide in high school students. *Journal of Adolescence, 36,* 341-350.

Bauman, S., Underwood, M. K. & Card, N. A. (2013). Definitions: Another perspective and a proposal for beginning with cyberaggression. In S. Bauman, D. Cross, & J. Walker (Eds.), *Principles of cyberbullying research: Definitions, measures, methodology,* (pp. 26-40). New York, NY: Routledge.

Bayar, Y. & Ucanok, Z. (2012). School social climate and generalized peer perception in traditional and cyberbullying status. *Educational Sciences: Theory & Practice, 12,* 2352-2358.

Beckman, L., Hagquist, C. & Hellstrom, L. (2012). Does the association with psychosomatic health problems differ between cyberbullying and traditional bullying? *Emotional and Behavioural Difficulties*, 17, 421-434.

Bonanno, R. A. & Hymel, S. (2013). Cyber bullying and internalizing difficulties: Above and beyond the impact of traditional forms of bullying. *Journal of Youth & Adolescence, 42,* 685-697.

Boulton, M., Lloyd, J., Down, J. & Marx, H. (2012). Predicting undergraduates' self-reported engagement in traditional and cyberbullying from attitudes. *Cyberpsychology, Behavior, and Social Networking, 15(3)*, 141-147.

Brighi, A., Guarini, A., Melotti, G., Galli, S. & Genta, M. L. (2012). Predictors of victimisation across direct bullying, indirect bullying and cyberbullying. *Emotional and Behavioural Difficulties, 17,* 375-388.

Burton, K. A., Florell, D. & Wygant, D. B. (2013). The role of peer attachment and normative beliefs about aggression on traditional bullying and cyberbullying. *Psychology in the Schools, 50,* 103-114.

Cappadocia, M. C., Craig, W. M. & Pepler, D. (2013). Cyberbullying: Prevalence, stability and risk factors during adolescence. *Canadian Journal of School Psychology, 28,* 171-192.

Cassidy, W., Brown, K. & Jackson, M. (2012a). "Making kind cool": Parents' suggestions for preventing cyber bullying and fostering cyber kindness. *Journal of Educational Computing Research, 46,* 415-436.

Cassidy, W., Brown, K. & Jackson, M. (2012b). "Under the radar": Educators and cyberbullying in schools. *School Psychology International, 33,* 520-532.

Corcoran, L., Connolly, I. & O'Moore, M. (2012). Cyberbullying in Irish schools: An investigation of *personality and self-concept. The Irish Journal of Psychology, 33,* 153-165.

Curelaru, M., Iacob, I. & Abalasei, B. (2009). *School bullying: Definition, characteristics, and intervention strategies.* Lumean Publishing House.

Dehue, F., Bolman, C. & Vollink, T. (2008). Cyberbullying: Youngsters' experiences and parental perception. *Cyber Pscyhology & Behavior, 11,* 217-223.

Dehue, F., Bolman, C., Vollink, T. &Pouwelse, M. (2012). Cyberbullying and traditional bullying in relation to adolescents' perceptions of parenting. *Journal of Cyber Therapy & Rehabilitation, 5,* 25-34.

deLara, E. W. (2012). Why adolescents don't disclose incidents of bullying and harassment. *Journal of School Violence, 11(4),* 288-305.

Diamanduros, T. & Downs, E. (2011). Creating a safe school environment: How to prevent cyberbullying at your school. *Library Media Connection, 30(2),* 36-38.

Eden, S., Heiman, T. & Olenik-Shemesh, D. (2013). Teachers' perceptions, beliefs and concerns about cyberbullying. *British Journal of Educational Technology, 44, 1036-1052.*

Elledge, L. C., Williford, A., Boulton, A. J., DePaolis, K. J., Little, T. D. & Salmivalli, C. (2013). Individual and contextual predictors of cyberbullying: The influence of children's provictim attitudes and teachers' ability to intervene. *Journal of Youth & Adolescence, 42,* 698-710.

Erdur-Baker, O. (2010). Cyberbullying and its correlation to traditional bullying, gender and frequent and risky usage of internet-mediated communication tools. *New Media & Society, 12,* 109-125.

Fanti, K. A., Demetriou, A. G. & Hawa, V. V. (2012). A longitudinal study of cyberbullying: Examining risk and protective factors. *European Journal of Developmental Psychology, 8,* 168-181.

Festl, R., Schwarkow, M. & Quandt, T. (2013). Peer influence, internet use and cyberbullying: A comparison of different context effects among German adolescents. *Journal of Children and Media, 7,* 446-462.

Goebert, D., Else, I., Matsu, C., Chung-Do, J. & Chang, J. Y. (2011). The impact of cyberbullying on substance use and mental health in a multiethnic sample. *Maternal Child Health Journal, 15,* 1282-1286.

Gradinger, P., Strohmeier, D. & Spiel, C. (2009). Traditional bullying and cyberbullying. *Journal of Psychology, 217,* 205-213.

Grigg, D. W. (2012). Definitional constructs of cyberbullying and cyber aggression from a triagnulatory overview: A preliminary study into elements. *Journal of Aggression, Conflict, and Peace Research, 4,* 202-215.

Hinduja, S. & Patchin, J. W. (2007). Offline consequences of online victimization. *Journal of School Violence, 6,* 89-112.

Hinduja, S. & Patchin, J. W. (2008). Cyberbullying: An exploratory analysis of factors related to offending and victimization. *Deviant Behavior, 29,* 129-156.

Hinduja, S. & Patchin, J. W. (2010). Bullying, cyberbullying, and suicide. *Archives of Suicide Research, 14,* 206-221.

Hinduja, S. & Patchin, J. W. (2012). Cyberbullying: Neither and epidemic nor a rarity. *European Journal of Developmental Psychology, 9,* 539-543.

Hinduja, S. & Patchin, J. W. (2013). Social influences on cyberbullying behaviors among middle and high school students. *Journal of Youth & Adolescence, 42,* 711-722.

Huang, Y. & Chou, C. (2010). An analysis of multiple factors of cyberbullying among junior high school students in Taiwan. *Computers in Human Behavior, 26,* 1581-1590.

Jang, H., Song, J. & Kim, R. (2014). Does the offline bully-victimization influence cyberbullying behavior among youths? Application of general strain theory. *Computers in Human Behavior, 31,* 85-93.

Joinson, A. (1998). Causes and implications of behavior on the Internet. In J. Gackenbach (Ed.), *Psychology and the Internet: Intrapersonal, interpersonal, and transpersonal implications,* (pp. 43-60). San Diego, CA: Academic Press.

Kochenderfer-Ladd, B. & Pelletier, M. (2008). Teachers' views and beliefs about bullying: Influences on classroom management strategies and students' coping with peer victimization. *Journal of School Psychology, 46,* 431-453.

Kowalski, R. M. & Limber, S. P. (2007). Electronic bullying among middle school students. *Journal of Adolescent Health, 41,* 22-30.

Kwan, G. C. E. & Skoric, M. M. (2013). Facebook bullying: An extension of battles in school. *Computers in Human Behavior, 29(1)*, 16-25.

Laftman, S. B., Modin, B. & Ostberg, V. (2013). Cyberbullying and subjective health: A large-scale study of students in Stockholm, Sweden. *Children and Youth Services Review, 35,* 112-119.

Lazuras, L., Barkoukis, V., Ourda, D. & Tsorbatzoudis, H. (2013). A process model of cyberbullying in adolescence. *Computers in Human Behavior, 29*, 881-887.

Lenhart, A. (2015). Teens, social media & technology overview 2015. Retrieved from: http://www.pewinternet.org/2015/04/09/teens-social-media-technology-2015/.

Li, Q. (2007). Bullying in the new playground: Research into cyberbullying and cyber victimization. *Australian Journal of Educational Technology, 23*, 435-454.

Li, Q. (2008). A cross-cultural comparison of adolescents' experience related to cyberbullying. *Educational Research, 50,* 223-234.

Machackova, H., Dedkova, L. & Mezulanikova, K. (2015). Brief report: The bystander effect in cyberbullying incidents. *Journal of Adolescence, 43,* 96-99.

Machackova, H., Dedkova, L., Sevcikova, A. & Cerna, A. (2013). Bystanders' support of cyberbullied schoolmates. *Journal of Community & Applied Social Psychology, 23(1)*, 25-36.

Mason, K. (2008). Cyberbullying: A preliminary assessment for school personnel. *Psychology in the Schools, 45,* 323-348.

McKenna, K. Y. A. & Bargh, J. A. (2000). Plan 9 from cyberspace: The implications of the internet for personality and social psychology. *Personality & Social Psychology Review, 4,* 57-75.

McQuade, C. S., Colt, P. J. & Meyer, B. N. (2009). *Cyber bullying: Protecting kids and adults from online bullies.* Westport: Praeger.

Mitchell, K. J., Ybarra, M. & Finkelhor, D. (2007). The relative importance of online victimization in understanding depression, delinquency, and substance use. *Child Maltreatment, 12,* 314-324.

Mouttapa, M., Valente, T., Gallagher, P., Rohrbach, L. A. & Unger, J. B. (2004). Social network predictor of bullying and victimization. *Adolescence, 39*, 315-335.

Olweus, D. (1993*). Bullying at school. What we know and what we can do.* Malden, MA: Blackwell Publishing.

Patchin, J. W. & Hinduja, S. (2006). Bullies move beyond the schoolyard: A preliminary look at cyberbullying. *Youth Violence and Juvenile Justice, 4*, 148-169.

Perren, S., Dooley, J., Shaw, T. & Cross, D. (2010). Bullying in school and cyberspace: Associations with depressive symptoms in Swiss and Australian adolescents. *Child and Adolescent Psychiatry and Mental Health, 4*, 1-10.

Pornari, C. D. & Wood, J. (2010). Peer and cyber aggression in secondary school students: The role of moral disengagement, hostile attribution bias, and outcome expectancies. *Aggressive Behavior, 36*, 81-94.

Rideout, V. J., Roberts, D. F. & Foehr, U. G. (2005). *Generation M: Media in the lives of 8-18-year-olds: Executive summary.* Menlo Park, CA: Henry J. Kaiser Family Foundation.

Rosen, L. D. (2007). *Me, Myspace, and I: Parenting the Net Generation.* New York: Palgrave Macmillan.

Sahin, M. (2010). Teachers' perceptions of bullying in high schools: A Turkish study. *Social Behavior and Personality, 38*, 127-142.

Sevcikova, A., Machackova, H., Wright, M. F., Dedkova, L. & Cerna, A. (2015). Social support seeking in relation to parental attachment and peer relationships among victims of cyberbullying. *Australian Journal of Guidance and Couselling, 15*, 1-13. doi: 10.1017/jgc.2015.1.

Shapka, J. D. & Law, D. M. (2013). Does one size fit all? Ethnic differences in parenting behaviors and motivations for adolescent engagement in cyberbullying. *Journal of Youth & Adolescence, 42*, 723-738.

Shariff, S. & Hoff, D. L. (2007). Cyber bullying: Clarifying legal boundaries for school supervision in cyberspace. *International Journal of Cyber Criminology, 1*, 76-118.

Sijtsema, J. J., Ashwin, R. J., Simona, C. S. & Gina, G. (2014). Friendship selection and influence in bullying and defending. *Effects of moral disengagement. Developmental Psychology*, *50*(8), 2093-2104.

Sjurso, I. R., Fandream, H. & Roland, E. (2016). Emotional problems in traditional and cyber victimization. *Journal of School Violence*, *15*(1), 114-131.

Smith, P. K., Del Barrio, C. & Tokunaga, R. S. (2013). Definitions of bullying and cyberbullying: How useful are the terms? In S. Bauman, D. Cross, & J. Walker (Eds.), *Principles of cyberbullying research: Definitions, measures, methodology*, (pp. 26-40). New York, NY: Routledge.

Smith, P. K., Mahdavi, J., Carvalho, M., Fisher, S., Russell, S. & Tippett, N. (2008). Cyberbullying: Its nature and impact in secondary school pupils. *Journal of Child Psychology and Psychiatry*, *49*, 376-385.

Sourander, A., Brunstein, A., Ikonen, M., Lindroos, J., Luntamo, T., Koskelainen, M., &Ristkari, T. & Helenius, H. (2010). Psychosocial risk factors associated with cyberbullying among adolescents: A population-based study. *Archives of General Psychiatry*, *67*, 720-728.

Stoll, L. C. & Block, R. (2015). Intersectionality and cyberbullying: A study of cyber victimization in a Midwestern high school. *Computers in Human Behaviors*, *52*, 387-391.

Strohmeier, D., Aoyama, I., Gradinger, P. & Toda, Y. (2013). Cyber victimization and cyber aggression in Eastern and Western countries: Challenges of constructing a cross-cultural appropriate scale. In S. Bauman, D. Cross, & J. L. Walker (Eds.), *Principles of cyberbullying research: Definitions, measures, and methodology*, (pp. 202-221). New York: Routledge.

Suler, J. (2004). The online disinhibition effect. *Cyber Psychology & Behavior*, *7*, 321-326.

Tangen, D. & Campbell, M. (2010). Cyberbullying prevention: One primary school's approach. *Australian Journal of Guidance & Counselling*, *20*, 225-234.

Toledano, S., Werch, B. L. & Wiens, B. A. (2015). Domain-specific self-concept in relation to traditional and cyber peer aggression. *Journal of School Violence, 14*(4), 405-423.

Totura, C. M. W., MacKinnon-Lewis, C., Gesten, E. L., Gadd, R., Divine, K. P., Dunham, S. & Kamboukos, D. (2009). Bullying and victimization among boys and girls in middle school: The influence of perceived family and school contexts. *The Journal of Early Adolescence, 29*, 571-609.

Wade, A. & Beran, T. (2011). Cyberbullying: The new era of bullying. *Canadian Journal of School Psychology, 26*, 44-61.

Wong, D. S., Chan, H. C. O. & Cheng, C. H. (2014). Cyberbullying perpetration and victimization among adolescents in Hong Kong. *Children and Youth Services Review, 36*, 133-140.

Wright, M. F. (in press). Adolescents' cyber aggression perpetration and cyber victimization: The longitudinal associations with school functioning. *Social Psychology of Education.*

Wright, M. F. (2013). The relationship between young adults' beliefs about anonymity and subsequent cyber aggression. *Cyber Psychology, Behavior, & Social Networking, 16*, 858-862.

Wright, M. F. (2014a). Cyber victimization and perceived stress: Linkages to late adolescents' cyber aggression and psychological functioning. *Youth & Society.*

Wright, M. F. (2014b). Predictors of anonymous cyber aggression: The role of adolescents' beliefs about anonymity, aggression, and the permanency of digital content. *Cyber Psychology, Behavior, & Social Networking, 17*, 431-438.

Wright, M. F. (2014c). Longitudinal investigation of the associations between adolescents' popularity and cyber social behaviors. *Journal of School Violence, 13*, 291-314.

Wright, M. F. (2015). Cyber victimization and adjustment difficulties: The mediation of Chinese and American adolescents' digital technology usage. *Cyber Psychology: Journal of Psychosocial Research in Cyberspace, 1*(1), article 1. Retrieved from: http://cyberpsychology.eu/view.php?cisloclanku=2015051102&article=1.

Wright, M. F., Kamble, S., Lei, K., Li, Z., Aoyama, I. & Shruti, S. (2015). Peer attachment and cyberbullying involvement among Chinese, Indian, and Japanese adolescents. *Societies, 5*, 339-353.

Wright, M. F. & Li, Y. (2012). Kicking the digital dog: A longitudinal investigation of young adults' victimization and cyber-displaced aggression. *Cyber Psychology, Behavior, & Social Networking, 15*, 448-454.

Wright, M. F. & Li. Y. (2013a). Normative beliefs about aggression and cyber aggression among young adults: A longitudinal investigation. *Aggressive Behavior, 39*, 161-170.

Wright, M. F. & Li, Y. (2013b). The association between cyber victimization and subsequent cyber aggression: The moderating effect of peer rejection. *Journal of Youth & Adolescence, 42*, 662-674.

Ybarra, M. L. & Mitchell, K. J. (2004). Online aggressor/targets, aggressors, and targets: A comparison of associated youth characteristics. *Journal of Child Psychology and Psychiatry, 45*, 1308-1316.

Ybarra, M. L., Diener-West, M. & Leaf, P. (2007). Examining the overlap in internet harassment and school bullying: Implications for school intervention. *Journal of Adolescent Health, 1*, 42-50.

Yousef, W. S. M. & Bellamy, A. (2015). The impact of cyberbullying on the self-esteem and academic functioning of Arab American middle and high school students. *Electronic Journal of Research in Educational Psychology, 23(3)*, 463-482.

Zhou, Z., Tang, H., Tian, Y., Wei, H., Zhang, F. & Morrison, C. M. (2013). *Cyberbullying and its risk factors among Chinese high school students. School Psychology International, 34*, 630-647.

In: Advances in Sociology Research   ISBN: 978-1-53616-781-8
Editor: Jared A. Jaworski   © 2020 Nova Science Publishers, Inc.

Chapter 4

USE OF MUSIC TECHNOLOGY FOR ENHANCING CHILDREN'S SOCIAL BEHAVIOURS: FINDINGS FROM A CASE-STUDY IN EAST LONDON, UK

*Tiija Rinta**

Department of Arts and Humanities, Institute of Education University
College London, London, UK

ABSTRACT

A considerable amount of research has been conducted on different art forms and their possible effect on social behaviours (Rinta et al., 2011). Such research has broadened our understanding of social behaviours and human nature (Welch, 2018). For instance, group music-making activities have been linked to enhanced ability to communicate (Welch et al., 2016). Currently, with the increasing use of music technology in education, there has been debate on the potential impact of technology on children's social behaviours (IIimonides et al., 2018). In order to investigate the issue further, a project was set up in East London (UK) that assessed the use of music technology as one of the primary

---

* Corresponding Author's Email: tiija.rinta@gmail.com.

tools in an extra-curricularmusic programme consisting of collaborative and individual music-making activities. In this chapter, we will describe the project in detail and outline its primary findings, with specific reference to its potential effect on children's social behaviours. The social context of the project is considered and how similar projects could potentially be implemented in other contexts.

INTRODUCTION

Musical behaviours can be recorded in all cultures, with various forms of music making or more passive musical participation recorded for different age-groups (Switala and Wyrskowska, 2018). For the young, engaging in musical activities with others can greatly enhance their sense of well-being and provide them with meaningful activities (Charissi and Rinta, 2014). However, the increasing use of music technology has raised concerns on its potentially isolating effect on the young, creating a feeling of uncertainty as to whether its use is of benefit or hindrance (Charissi and Rinta, op.cit.).

In this chapter, we outline and discuss a recent music education project that took place in East London (UK) and how the use of a music making application was utilized in enhancing the young participant's social behaviours and in increasing their perceived sense of social inclusion. The findings from the project provide encouraging evidence for engaging in music and positive ways of using music technology with the young that reduce their feelings of isolation and enhance their social behaviours.

MUSIC AND ITS SOCIAL NATURE

Learning in groups or during individual lessons is at all times a social process that requires cooperation, with participants interacting by playing in freely created ensembles, or with the educator (Switala and Wyrsykowska, 2018). In this respect, music appears to be a special subject, as listening to others is a key aspect of any musical activity (Elliott, 2015).

Hence, by practicing music, children should always develop their social skills (Switala and Wyrsykowska, 2018).

Social-emotional development has been found to be enhanced by music education and when engaging in musical activities (Kupana, 2015). Moreover, music and social-emotional learning complement each other in the education process with the following properties: a.) Music can be used as an emotional stimulus; b.) Music can be used as an aesthetic experience; c.) Music can be used for relaxation and imagination; d.) Making music can be a form of self expression; and e.) Making music can be a form of group experience (Kupana, op.cit.).

Furthermore, musical behaviours can be recorded in young infants even prior to their ability to speak coherently (Gerry et al., 2012). Such musical behaviours and their impact on general development can be facilitated and encouraged through appropriate musical pedagogical approaches, in additional enhancing culture-specific musical acquisition and social as well as communication development (Gerry et al., op.cit.). Similar findings have been reported with adolescents and emphasis has been placed on the developmental importance of music in this age-group (Dave, 2012).

SOCIAL SKILLS AND MUSIC AS THERAPY

For children who possess limited verbal communication skills, music can function as a means for self-expression and mutual communication (Hongisto-Åberg et al., 1993). Shared music making requires several social skills (such as sharing, copying ideas and taking turns) (Hongisto-Aberg et al., 2007). Music therapy is a unique form of therapy, yet it shares the same goals as speech and language therapy (Ala-Ruona et al., op.cit.). This form of therapy can be used for facilitating communication, self-expression, emotion regulation and for enhancing concentration (Ala-Ruona et al., 2007). As stated by Bruscia (1998), music can be used for a number of non-therapeutic outcomes.

As a result of improved scientific experiments (such as electronic magnetic imaging), a more comprehensive understanding of how music influences our being can be formulated and its application to therapy enhanced (Särkämö and Huotilainen, 2012). Neuroscience has generated new knowledge on how the human brain processes music and provided detail on the neural basis for how music in therapy can influence us. Music activates a large section of neural pathways in the brain that crossed over from the right hemisphere to the left. This area is responsible for a number of functions, including auditory, emotional, cognitive and motor functions (Bruscia, 1998).

In therapy, music is a useful and helpful stimuli for enhancing communication (Särkämö and Huotilainen, 2012). Music can evoke a wide range of emotional responses in individuals, potentially to a greater extent than any other stimuli. Furthermore, music can help one with focussing and concentration, and it can energise or relax (Charissi and Rinta, 2011). Moreover, music can improve one's memory. Music and speech are both forms of communication that utilise the acoustic features of sound (such as auditory pitch, real-time features and the tone of sound) (Dave, 2012). Music has been found to be effective in treating a number of language disorders (such as deaf children who possess limited verbal communication skills due to a lack of auditory feedback) (Tallal and Gaab, 2006; Torppa and Huotilainen, 2010). Moreover, singing specifically has been found to be effective in treating individuals with neurological disorders (such as Parkinson's, stuttering and patients with brain damage) (Wan et al., 2010).

A few studies have established a link between musical interventions and socially responsive behaviours. For instance, a music therapy intervention was found to increase three different kinds of social responsive behaviours in two separate therapy trials when compared to a more traditional therapy approach, suggesting that the music condition was more motivating for the participant than the non-music condition (Finnigan and Starr, 2010). Another example is the use of music in various forms (such as in composition, performance and improvisation) with adolescents who have emotional disorders, as a tool to provide a safe, non-confrontational means of expression, offering them with a more socially acceptable way of releasing anger and expressing their fears, and increasing the level of their perceived self-awareness, self-confidence and self-esteem (Keen, 2008). Similar results have been found on projects utilising school-based art interventions. Richard and colleagues (2012) reported that school-based music classes prevented a decline in self-esteem measures as well as in academic self-esteem.

MUSIC, TECHNOLOGY AND IMPACT ON SOCIAL BEHAVIOURS

Currently, the music industry utilizes digital technology in a wide range of applications, including performance, composition and in recording and publishing (Wise et al., 2011). A great deal of such technology is freely available via downloads from the internet, as part of software included with computers when purchased and via applications available formobile phones (Wise et al., op.cit.). Such technology is transforming the area of music and the way people approach a number of traditional music activities in and outside of school.

Over the past decade with the increasing use of music technology, there has been a great deal of debate on whether music technology is more of a hindrance or facilitator in children's musical development and its impact on children's overall development. Mixed results have been reported on this issue. A large-scale study conducted in three different European countries yielded positive results on the use of music technology with children by highlighting how, with the use of appropriate music technology in a classroom, children's musical and social skills can be developed (Charissi and Rinta, 2014).

Recent studies highlight that the manner in which technology and digital tools are used significantly influence the results. For instance, social networking platforms can be used for creating connections, sharing one's music and for learning (Salavuo, 2008). A student-centred approach to learning can also be created by offering ownership of the environment to its primary users through creating a need to communicate and contribute to a community of practice (Salavuo, op.cit.).

Despite recent research on music technology, it is yet unclear as to how its use might impact young people's social behaviours. The current project yielded some results in this regard.

CURRENT PROJECT

The current project took place in the Borough of Hackney in north-east London. Hackney is known for its multicultural demographics, with a mix of people from different European countries, Jamaica, Ghana and Nigeria forming the majority of the population. A decade ago, Hackney had a reputation of being a rough part of the city, with a number of gangs and gang-related crimes regularly being reported.

Over the past ten years, this part of London has developed immensely and become a sought-to-be place for hipsters and young artists in particular. A considerable amount of Government funding was invested into the area prior to the 2012 London Olympic Games, thanks to which the area has transformed itself. Despite the recent economic growth, Hackney still faces significant problems of poverty and inequality. The poverty rate in 2019 is 36%, well above the London average of 27%, and 5.4% of working age people are unemployed.

Nevertheless, the past two years have seen a surge in violent crimes, more specifically knife-related attacks. The increase in such violent crimes has become a severe concern for locals. A number of interventions to prevent the young from falling into crime has been set up by the local Government (such as programmes of mentoring through sport and apprenticeships with various organisations). There has been much debate on how to engage the young and offer them with meaningful activities in order to keep them motivated, focussed and out of criminal paths.

Our project was located in an area called Hackney Wick in the southern part of the borough. This area is home to a great number of creative industries and art studios. It is situated right next to the Olympic

Park that was specially developed for the 2012 London Olympic Games. However, it is also an old industrial estate where a significant number of residents worked in factories until about a decade ago when the factories started to close down. Despite the wide range of sporting venues and creative industries in the area, the shift from an industrial area to a more trendy creative area left a number of adults unemployed. This, in turn, has created a feeling of apprehension amongst the young who are fearful of their future and afraid of ending up unemployed once leaving education. As a result, a number of the young people lack motivation to pursue their chosen careers unless they have clear guidance on how to pursue such paths outside of their home boroughs. Such negative feelings have been found to be linked to lower feelings of social inclusion and deteriorated social behaviours (Rinta et al., 2011).

The aim of our project was to offer the local young people an opportunity to engage in musical activities that could potentially enhance their perceived feelings of social inclusion and improve their social behaviours. It was set up as a well-being project, whilst also offering the participants with the opportunity to develop musically and to learn about possible future careers in the field of music. The project was delivered at a local community centre and the participants were from local secondary schools.

PARTICIPANTS

In total, 39 children aged 11-15 formed the participant group. The participants were from school years 7 to 10 during the school year of 2018-2019. Twenty of the participants werefemale and nineteen were male. The participants were all local residents in the area of Hackney Wick in East London (UK). They attended three different local schools that were all state run, mainstream secondary schools. Two of the schools had been rated 'Outstanding' by the Government assessment body and one as 'Good'. The schools that the participants came from were selected purely due to their locality and relevance.

Two months prior to commencing the project, it was advertised via a local community centre, as well as directly with local schools in order to reach a wide range of local young people. Leaflets were given to parents and pupils after school hours at the schools and during community activities at the community centre. Permission was sought from the community centre and school staff for advertising. The centre and schools were all supportive of the project and expressed no concern over the project when it was explained to them.

The participants came from a variety of ethnic backgrounds. The participants identified themselves as: white British or European (39%); black African or Caribbean (31%); Asian (19%); and a mixed ethnic background (11%). A mix of religions was also recorded: 25% were Christian; 22% were Muslim; 16% were Hindu; 8% Jewish; and 29% reported no religion. According to the traditional class classification frequently applied in the UK, the participants came from different socioeconomic backgrounds, with 36% being classed as living in poverty.

ETHICS

Ethical guidelines of the British Educational Research Association (BERA) and the Hackney Local Government were followed throughout the study. Parental and teacher approval was requested prior to commencing any data collection. Initially, the Head teachers of the schools and the Manager of the community centre were contacted. A letter was sent to the parents of the participants in order to request approval for their child to participate in the study.

The teachers, parents and participants children were reassured of confidentiality issues and they were informed that the data were to be used for the current study only and not to be passed on to a third party. The project manager had undergone a criminal bureau check (CRBC) prior to commencing the study in order to be able to conduct the experiments with the children on her own.

METHODS

The project was run for one school term (Spring term: January to March 2018-2019). The sessions took place three times a week (Monday, Wednesday and Friday late afternoons) for 75 minutes each time, requiring a substantial commitment from participants as they were expected to attend all sessions if at all possible. A hub for music-making was set up in the local community centre that was an easily accessible location for all participants who lived close to it in the local area.

Each of the three weekly sessions had a specific focus and were unique in nature:

(a) Session One on Mondays consisted of group music-making with singing, easy-to-play percussion instruments (such as hand drums) and simple string instruments (such as the ukulele);

(b) Session Two on Wednesdays focussed on using music technology in music making on computers, tablets and digital musical instruments; and

(c) Session Three on Fridays provided opportunities to use specific music composition programmes with traditional musical instruments (such as a piano keyboard or guitar) with the aim to improvise and to compose music in a small group setting.

In addition to the sessions, the participants had access to an online platform for sharing musical ideas outside of the music sessions. The platform included a 12 hour chat room (daily from 8am to 8pm) that was monitored by the project manager. All participants were provided with usernames and passwords for the site and were assured of confidentiality concerns.

DESCRIPTION OF SESSIONS

The three weekly sessions were each unique in their approach to music making. Below are more detailed descriptions of each type of session.

(a) Session One on Mondays

Session One on Mondays adapted a more traditional approach to making music. The only piece of technology used in this session was a recording device that was used to record the final performance of the day. This enabled the participants to keep an audio diary of their Monday evening music sessions. At the end of each session, the participants had a chance to share their musical creations in their online chat room space.

Each of the Monday evening sessions utilized different types traditional musical instruments over the 12 week duration of the project. The first session was focused on simple string instruments (such as ukulele and guitar). The second session utilized keyboard and piano. The third session used simple percussion instruments (such as hand drums and castanets). The fourth session was primarily focussed on vocals and singing in a small group, with support from piano and guitar. The succession of the four sessions was repeated twice in order to provide the participants with opportunities to develop their music making skills with traditional musical instruments.

(b) Session Two on Wednesdays

Sessions Two on Wednesdays focussed on using technology in music making. Sibelius and Garage Band were used in creating music, as they were well-known programme frequently used in education settings with the concerned age-group (Charissi and Rinta, 2014). The software was used on tablets and computers. In the first Wednesday session, the participants were introduced to the software and shown how it worked. They were provided with an opportunity to try the software in order to familiarize themselves with it.

Once the participants were familiar with the software, each subsequent Wednesday session adapted a theme to focus on (such as creating new compositions or improvisation based on a musical lead). Since the design of the programme provided a structured yet flexible approach to creating and making music, the sessions were treated as open spaces where the participants could use the software in such a manner. In comparison to the Monday sessions, the Wednesday sessions were more open and 'freestyle' in nature.

(c) Session Three on Fridays

The aim of Session Three on Fridays was to combine the approaches used in Session One on Monday with those used in Session Two on Wednesday. Technology was used as the main tool in both composition and general music making activities, with traditional musical instruments being played on top of backing tracks from the selected software programmes, or leads and loops for composition being provided by the software.

The sessions were designed to be as open-ended as possible with minimal structure in order to allow space for creativity and for musical ideas to shape and grow. The participants were encouraged to engage in music creation and making in small groups, but at times they engaged in music making individually and subsequently shared their musical creations with their group at the end of the session and online in their chat room.

PROCEDURE

The sessions all started with a warm up activity. This activity lasted for the first ten minutes of the session and enabled the participants to feel comfortable and relaxed prior to commencing music making. The warm up activities consisted of singing simple melodies, or playing percussion instruments when a participant preferred this to singing. The following 55 minutes were dedicated to the primary activity of the session. The timeframe was deemed suitable in order to allow sufficient space for the intended musical activity. The final ten minutes of the session were used for a cooling down activity. This consisted of listening to relaxing music in comfortable meditation style positions.

Two project workers were present throughout the sessions and ensured that all participants understood what to do and assisted as appropriate. The sessions were videoed on the participants' consent and the video footage was subsequently analysed.

PRE- AND POST-ASSESSMENT

Social Inclusion Assessment

Pre-and post-assessment of the participants' feelings of social inclusion was carried out in order to determine whether the project activities appeared to yield positive results in this regard. In addition, demographics and information on musical learning were gathered via a simple survey prior and subsequent to the project sessions.

A newly formulated instrument for assessing social inclusion was adapted to the study (Rinta et al., 2011). The assessment instrument had been used in a number of multicultural settings in different countries and had been found to be a valid and reliable instrument for the intended purpose (Charissi and Rinta, 2014). On average, it took approximately eight minutes for the participants to be assessed with the use of the social inclusion instrument.

Social Behaviour Assessment

The participants' social behaviours were assessed via video analyses and live observation. Likert-scales were adapted to the assessment instruments in order to be able to analyse the data quantitatively. Assessment was carried out by two different observers and the data were meaned prior to analyses. The observers had a clear and comprehensive understanding of what was expected of them during the task and the manner in which the assessment was to be carried out.

The behavioural aspects that were specifically placed emphasis on were: initiative to communicate; amount of time in minutes spent conversing with peers or leaders; and amount of time in minutes spent working in group activities. Such aspects were regarded as basic skills forming the basis of a significant number of social behaviour (Finnigan and Starr, 2010).

Musical Composition Assessment

The participants' musical engagement and compositions were assessed with the use of the Swanick-Tillman spiral model for musical development (Rinta et al., 2011). The model offered a straightforward and concise assessment method for musical creations and development, and it had been found to be a reliable, effective and valid assessment tool in previous studies (Rinta et al., 2011).

Survey

At the end of the project, a survey was carried out with the participants in order to gather more detailed information on their perceptions on the programme sessions. The survey items focussed on perceived sense of social inclusion and social behaviours, and whether there were any perceived changes in this regard, as well as musical behaviours and identity. The participants were also inquired about their friendships, how often and how much they communicated and engaged with their peers and those around them, as well as their sense of belonging to their communities.

Review of Online Chat Room Activity

The activity of the online chat room was logged and analysed qualitatively in order to determine whether it had changed over time. Emphasis was placed on the amount of chatting that took place in the chat rooms and its contents, in particular the quality of conversation around musical engagement and sharing of one's own musical creations.

DATA ANALYSES

All sessions were video recorded for data analysis purposes. Permission for this wasobtained from the children's parents, as well as from the school. One of the project workers who was an academically trained researcher also observed the sessions and recorded observed findings on an observation sheet.

Data gathered via observation and video-recording were analysed qualitatively. Data gathered via the social inclusion instrument, the music background questionnaire and the survey were analysed quantitatively. Data gathered from the children's compositions were also analysed quantitatively with software that analysed the loops of the compositions.

RESULTS

Sense of Social Inclusion and Enhanced Social Behaviours

One-way ANOVAs were used in the analysis with the data gathered using the social inclusion instrument and the background questionnaire. The data were entered intoan Excel-file.

The most significant finding was that the pupils felt more socially-included subsequent to the project sessions compared to prior to them ($p<0.05$). In particular, statistically significant differences ($p<0.05$) were recorded for the following items: 'I can be sure my friends take my side if I have an argument.'; 'Having a few really close friends is more important than trying to be friends with everybody.'; 'I would be sad if I had to leave my school.';' Other children like me just the way I am.'; and 'I like to see my school friends outside school.'. The pupils agreed with the above statements more strongly subsequent to the project sessions.

The video footage from the sessions was analysed by the project team. In the analysis, specific attention was paid to social behaviour of the pupils and any psychological benefits that seemed to arise from the sessions. The majority of the participants worked effectively and engaged in significant social activity during the project sessions. In particular, a great deal of talking was recorded between the participants, including: sharing ideas; giving advice; and suggestions (such as: 'Try that icon.', 'The music from that picture sounded very nice.', 'Well done, that's great'.).

Although caution is needed in the interpretation that the finding as a direct outcome of participation in the project activities, an increase in social skills and behavior throughout the project was recorded, as evidenced in the video recording and observations, as well as reported by the concerned adults and the pupils themselves. Such behaviours included: talking with one another; collaboration; sharing of ideas; working in pairs; encouraging comments made towards one's partner; working in groups; and willingness to share compositions with the rest of the group. The project workers observed that at least some of the pupils who were generally quiet and did not interact with their peers demonstrated a wider range of social skills as a result of the sessions. Moreover, many of the pupils considered as more socially excluded at the start of the project also enthusiastically engaged in the activity (including immigrant and SEN children).

Pearson correlations were calculated between the responses received for the music questions and the meaned social inclusion ratings. Four statistically significant findings were recorded:

(a) the higher the number of days per week that the participants engaged in the project activities, the more socially included they felt (p<0.05; 0.003);

(b) the higher the number of days per week that the participants shared their musical creations in the online chat room with their peers, the more socially included they felt (p<0.05; 0.001);

(c) the higher the number of days per week that the participants engaged in out of project musical activities, the more socially included they felt (p<0.05, 0.001); and

(d) the higher the number of days per week that the participants received music education at school, the more socially included the they felt (p<0.05; 0.045).

Improved Musical Development and Creations

Compositions were produced by the participants as part of the project. They were shared in the sessions and also in the online chat room. In total, there were 108 compositions produced over the project sessions and they varied in their levels of musical sophistication and in their adoption of common musical conventions. However, the majority appeared to fall within reasonably predictable age-ranges on the well-established Swanwick-Tillman 'spiral' model of musical development (Swanick, 1988).

The children's perceptions of musical activities were more positive subsequent to the project sessions than prior to them (p<0.05). Particularly significant statistical differences were recorded for the following musical statements: 'I like doing musical activities very much'; 'For me, being given a chance to take part in musical activities is very important'; and 'I enjoy the musical activities I currently do'.

The children reported that they enjoyed musical activities to a greater extent after having had a chance to engage musically in the project sessions. Comments by the children on such activities included:

'It was mint to do stuff with the music app. It's so cool that I want all my friends to do it too.' Boy, 11, Somali

'I never did this good music activities before. It is much more fun than some other music stuff we do.' Girl, 12, Afghani

'I like music activities more now. I never used to do much of them, but now I know I can.' Boy, 14, Iraqi

'I never used any kind of technology to make music before. It is ace!' Boy, 13, English

'It was fun. I think I can do a lot more with computers now and enjoy it too.' Girl, 15, Jamaican

'I play more with my own phone and computer now. I think I know now how I can enjoy music more.' Girl, 13, Nigerian

An improvement in the complexity of the compositions was recorded over the duration of the project. Initially, the majority of the participants composed with the use of one to three instruments, yet towards the end, the majority had added another two instruments that, on the whole, resulted in compositions utilizing rhythmic, melodic and background instruments in addition to vocals. Furthermore, a greater variety in tonality and rhythmic changes was recorded towards the end of the project.

As the project progressed, the number of comments and communication in the chat room with reference to individual musical compositions increased considerably. In the first week of the project, only eight participants signed into the chat room and provided feedback to their peers. In the final week, all participants signed into the chat room and provided feedback for more than three other participants.

Improved Friendships

All of the participants reported that their friendships had improved over the course of the project. 14 of the participants had reported not having strong friendships prior to the project, yet they had managed to make new friends in the project sessions. Others (N=25) reported having had strong friendships prior to the project, yet they felt that they had formed valuable new friendships during the project.

A sense of improved friendships, in turn, appeared to enhance the participant's feelings of social inclusion and belonging. Below are a few examples of how the participants felt about their improved friendships:

> *'I had friends before the project, but I made more firm friendships during the project sessions.'* Girl, 15, English

> *'I love the new friends I have made during the project. We have so much in common.'* Boy, 13, Ghanaian

> *'I made new friends that I can talk to any time. They understand me.'* Girl, 12, Chinese

During the project, the participants established firm friendships with other participants and arranged to see each other outside of the project sessions. The participants perceived their newly formed friendships in a positive light and stated that they felt a stronger connection with their new friends due to their common interest in music.

> *'I like spending time with my new friends, because we can play and make music together.'* Boy, 11, South Asian

> *'My new friends listen to the same type of music as me so we can talk about it.'* Girl, 13, French

> *'I have more in common with my new friends, though I still see my old friends too.'* Boy, 15, Spanish

> *'We can talk about music and make music together, which has given me more meaningful activities to my life.'* Girl, 15, English

Improved Participation in Musical Activities in and Out of School

A further positive outcome from the project was that the participants reported to be taking part in a greater number of musical activities subsequent to the project than prior to it. All of the participants reported that they had found new enjoyment in engaging in musical activities and found them more accessible, resulting in taking part in a greater number of musical activities in school and out of school. Out of the participants, 45% stated that they had started learning to play a new musical instrument during or subsequent to the project. An additional 14% reported that they had started singing in a choir or small group.

Furthermore, all of the participants stated that they had continued making music with technological devices and sharing their creations online with their friends. This was enabled by the co-ordinator of the group having set up a closed facebook group for the participants subsequent to the project. The applications and programmes that the participants reported to be using included: Garage Band; Logic; Piano Tiles; and Sibelius. The majority (90%) stated that they preferred using software used in the project to create music as they had become used to using it during the project.

On average, the participants spent one hour and eight minutes a day in music making or creating activities, primarily after school hours. In addition, the majority (90%) reported having increased their participation in music clubs and lessons at school. All of the participants stated that they felt that their musical skills had developed considerably over the duration of the project and this, in turn, had given the participants confidence to engage in a greater number of musical activities and in a more meaningful and self-fulfilling manner. The feedback from the participants highlighted the positive feelings that the project had created, as quoted below:

'Before the project, I wasn't sure if I was musical. But then we made a lot of nice music during the project and I realized that I can do it.' Girl, 13, English

'I never had a chance to learn how to use technology to make music. I needed to be taught during the project to get me started and now all I want to do is make music.' Boy, 14, Caribbean

'I feel great, because now I know that I can make music and be good at it and also make friends. It really has made me feel better about myself.' Girl, 12, Polish

'I have learnt to play different musical instruments and to enjoy creating my own music. I never thought that this would be possible.' Boy, 16, English

DISCUSSION

Despite the positive outcomes of the project, caution should be taken when interpreting the results. The statistical correlations and the descriptive data illustrated that the project yielded various positive outcomes, including amongst others: enhanced social behaviours and perceived sense of social inclusion; improved music making and creations; and a greater number of friendships. Nevertheless, it should be noted that other projects might also yield similar results. For instance, projects utilising different forms of art that bring the young together might result in similar positive outcomes. In order to investigate any potential differences between projects, a comparative study should be conducted. Yet, we cannot dismiss the apparent power of making and creating music, simply engaging in musical activities and enjoying music. As indicated in previous research studies (e.g., Keen, 2008; Rinta et al., 2011; Wan et al., 2010), music can have a powerful effect on humans. The current project provided further evidence on how musical engagement can potentially enhance social behaviours and feelings of social inclusion. Overall, the project had a very positive outcome, even when we cannot state that this would be the only type of project to generate such results.

It might be that the communal nature and structure of the project played a role in generating such positive results. The overall design of the project might have been a key element in generating the positive results. Similar projects that build on group activities and creative outlets could be implemented with young people in order to enhance their social behaviours and sense of social inclusion. The social nature of the project sessions might have played a crucial role in facilitating such positive improvement in the measured outcomes, with music functioning as a medium.

Previous research has indicated that group activities inevitably require communication and, consequently, more frequently than not result in enhanced social behaviours (such as improved ability to communicate and initiate contact with others) (Finnigan and Starr, 2010; Kupana, 2015; Rinta et al., 2011). Even though a variety of group activities appear to facilitate positive change in social behaviours, it should be noted that music activities (as part of a group or engage in individually) appear to facilitate enhancement in social behaviours, potentially as a direct result of enhanced feelings of belonging and heightened self-esteem (Rinta et al., op.cit.). The current project sheds further light on how music making with the use and help of technology can also enhance such behaviours.

In the current project, the online chat room proved to be a crucial element. It provided the participants with a safe space for sharing their musical creations and for communicating with their new friends. It might be that the online community boosted the participants' self-esteem, further enabling them to communicate more effectively offline. It might be that online activity and the use of technology, when it enables the young to link with their friends, has a more positive effect on their social behaviours and skills than previously thought. However, in order to investigate such initial findings further, a wider and bigger study is needed. A comparative study with one group utilising technology and another relying on more conventional methods would provide further evidence on the role of technology-based activities in enhancing social behaviour.

A strong emerging theme from the current study was a sense of belonging to a community. Humans have an innate desire to belong to a community and to be a part of a wider group of fellow humans (Tallal and Gaab, 2006; Wan et al., 2010). In today's society, a significant number of young people feel isolated and segregated in their communities, further leading to mental health problems (such as depression and anxiety) (Charissi and Rinta, 2014). Interventions are needed that reach to the young and assist them in feeling included in their communities (Charissi and Rinta et al., op.cit.). The current project certainly appeared to fill this role and provided the young with a community that further resulted in enhanced well-being, feelings of social inclusion and general positive feelings towards oneself. On the whole, the participants reported that the project had made a difference to how they felt about themselves and to how they belonged to their local community. The current project appeared to be a needed intervention in the local area, in particular at a time when knife crime was on the rise.

Moreover, an appealing motivating factor is needed for drawing young people in and for making them interested in any project. This seems to be of even more importance with adolescents (Kupana, 2015). Teenagers frequently prove to be a tough crowd to draw into any project, which warrants even more reason for planning and designing a project consisting of elements that would motivate the young to participate (Richard et al., 2012). In the current project, music functioned as such a motivating factor. In general, the young take an interest in at least popular music. Musical activities certainly proved to be effective in drawing young people in and in maintaining their motivation to take part in the project activities. In the context and locality of the project, music appeared to fulfil the role of a motivational factor extremely well. It should be noted that alternative motivation factors might work more effectively in other settings. For instance, sport activities or other creative arts might work more effectively in other settings.

Finally, the technology used in the project did not hinder the development of social behaviours and nor affect feelings of social inclusion negatively.However, it is unclear whether there would have been even more improvement in the specified areas if technology had not been used at all. In the future, a comparative study between a project utilizing technology and another one not utilising technology could provide further clarity on the issue.

REFERENCES

Ala-Ruona, E., Saukko, P.& Tarkki, A. (2007). *Services in music therapy.* Finland: The Music Therapy Association.

Bruscia, K. E. (1998). *Defining music therapy.* Spain: Barcelona Publishers.

Charissi, V. & Rinta, T. (2014). Children's musical and social behaviours in the context of music-making activities supported by digital tools: examples from a pilot study in the United Kingdom. *Journal of Music, Technology & Education, 7* (1), 39-58.

Dave, M. (2013). The role of music in adolescent development: much more than the same old song. *International Journal of Adolescence and Youth, 18*(1), 5-22.

Elliott, D. J. & Silverman, M.(2015).*Music matters: a philosophy of music education (2nd Ed.).* New York: Oxford University Press.

Finnigan, E. & Starr, E. (2010). Increasing social responsiveness in a child with autism: a comparison of music and non-music interventions. *Autism, 14*(4), 321-348.

Gerry, D., Unrau, A. & Trainor, L. J. (2012). Active music classes in infancy enhance musical, communicative and social development. *Annals of the New York Academy of Sciences, 15* (3), 398-407.

Hongisto-Åberg, M., Lindeberg-Piiroinen, A. & Mäkinen, L. (1993). *Music in early years education: handbook.* Finland: Fazer Music.

Keen, A. W. (2008). Using music as a therapy tool to motivate troubled dolescents. *Social Work in Health Care, 39* (3-4), 361-373.

Kupana, N. (2015). Social emotional learning and music education. *Sed, 3*(2), 75-88.

Richard, N. S., Appelman, P. & James, R. (2012). Orchestrating life skills: the effect of increased school-based music classes on children's social competence and self-esteem. *International Journal of Music Education, 31*(3), 292-309.

Rinta, T., Purves, R. & Welch, G. (2011). Usability of a jamming mobile with 3-6 year-old children for enhancing feelings of social inclusion and facilitating musical learning. *Proceedings from the 5th Conference of the European Network of Music Educators and Researchers of Young Children (MERYC2011),*Metropolia University of Applied Sciences, Helsinki, Finland, 8-11, June 2011.

Salavuo, M. (2008). Social media as an opportunity for pedagogical change in music education. *Journal of Music, Technology & Education, 1*(2-3), 121-136.

Särkämö, T. & Huotilainen, M. (2012). Music for the brain throughout life. *The Finnish Medical Journal, 17*(1), 1334–1339.

Swanwick, K. (1988). *Music, mind and eduction.* London, UK: Routledge.

Switala, A. & Wyrsykowska, K. (2019). *Participatory approach in music education and its influences on social behaviour and participation in culture.* Retrieved online 2 April 2019, https://www.researchgate.net/publication/322527125.

Tallal, P. & Gaab, N. (2006). Dynamic auditory processing, musical experience and language development. *Trends in Neurosciences, 29*(4), 382–390.

Torppa, R. & Huotilainen, M. (2010). The significance of music in the rehabilitation of children with hearing problems. *Speech and Language, 30*(2), 137–155.

UNESCO. (2019). *Education for all.* Retrieved online 1 May 2019, http://www.unesco.org/en/efa/the-efa-movement.

Wan, C. Y., Demaine, K., Zipse, L., Norton, A. & Schlauga, G. (2010). From music making to speaking: engaging the mirror neuron system in autism. *Brain Research Bulletin, 82*(4), 161 – 168.

Wise, Stuart., Greenwood, Janinka.& Davis, Niki. (2011). "Teachers' Use of Digital Technology in Secondary Music Education: Illustrations of Changing Classrooms". *British Journal of Music Education, 28*(2), 117-134.

In: Advances in Sociology Research
Editor: Jared A. Jaworski

ISBN: 978-1-53616-781-8
© 2020 Nova Science Publishers, Inc.

Chapter 5

EDUCATED WOMEN AS GATEKEEPERS TO PREVENT SEXUAL EXPLOITATION OF CHILDREN

Marika Guggisberg[*]*, PhD and Eva Dobozy, PhD*
[1]CQ University and Queensland Centre for Domestic
and Family Violence Research, Perth, Western Australia
[2]Curtin University, Perth, Western Australia

ABSTRACT

Online technologies have changed the lives of children and their families. They create countless benefits including for education, health, recreation and connecting people in removing physical barriers. However, these new ways of social networking bring with them unique risks. Women are uniquely positioned as gatekeepers to protect children from sexual exploitation and other forms of victimisation. This chapter examines online risks children may encounter including *content risk* such as online video games and *contact risk* related to sexting and sexual solicitation. The importance of awareness and education is emphasised along with future directions to ensure children are protected while participating in the online space.

---

[*] Corresponding Author's Email: m.guggisberg@cqu.edu.au.

Keywords: cyber, digital literacy, online technology, risk, sexting, solicitation

INTRODUCTION

Women remain the primary care givers of their own and other children in a variety of functions with taking around three times more time when compared to men (Australian Human Rights Commission, 2019). Furthermore, education is still a very gendered profession with the vast majority of teachers being female. Consequently, women are uniquely positioned as gatekeepers to protect children from danger and risk that arises from online technology. This includes sexualised content and interaction with known and unknown persons. For women, teaching children to be cyber safe is more important than ever. Mothers, aunts, friends, education and other professionals have a unique opportunity to protecting vulnerable children while they participate in the online space. This includes being informed and teaching children about the benefits and dangers of the internet.

INTERNET

The internet (information and communication technologies), which has been defined as 'a worldwide system of interconnected networks and computers' (Peter, 2004, n. p.), certainly changed how individuals interact (Smith & Grabosky, 2012). While its origins are debated, there is wide agreement that the internet created countless benefits including for recreation, education, health and connecting people in removing physical barriers. However, this advancement also provides unprecedented opportunities for sexual and other crimes (Smith & Grabosky, 2012; Schulz, Bergen, Schuhmann, Hoyer, & Santtila, 2016; Ybarra, Espelage, & Mitchell, 2007). Identifying and protecting vulnerable individuals, which of course includes children, poses a unique and new challenges today and for the years to come.

It is well known that children represent a growing proportion of internet users (Kumar et al., 2017; Livingstone, Carr, & Byrne, 2015). Even young children aged three and four years engage with online technology daily. In fact, evidence suggests that at the age of five years, children spend about three hours online every day, which includes on average one hour spent on mobile devices to play video games (James, Weinstein & Mendoza, 2019). With increasing age, children spend more time online with an average of six hours at the age of eight years and nine hourswhen they reach 13 years.

The new ways of social networking bring with them exciting opportunities, but also unique risks such as sexual contacts with known and unknown persons (Livingstone & Smith, 2014). Recently, concerns in relation to online risks to children have been raised in Australia, Europe, and the US to reduce sexual harm to those vulnerable minors (Schulz, et al., 2016), while at the same time acknowledging that online participation has become recognised as a human right.

ONLINE PARTICIPATION IS A HUMAN RIGHT

No-one argues against children having a right to express themselves online (Livingstone, et al., 2015). Children have the right to education including digital knowledge and protection, including being free of sexual abuse and exploitation. These principles are set out in the Universal Declaration on Human Rights (UDHR) and other international instruments by the UNCRC (Livingstone et al., 2015). Consequently, children's rights to online engagement can be explained as freedom to participate, while at the same time having the right to be protected from sexual and other forms of harm, which isa human right in the digital age. This includes being informed about concepts such as 'digital footprint.'

Digital Footprint

Children explore their online identities and express themselves online including choosing specific avatars when playing video games. Once they are older, this behaviour extends to interacting with others more personally including snapping selfies and posting information including live broadcasting of images and videos. These actions make up their unique digital footprint, which is a trail of all their online activities (James et al., 2019). Children often use multiple accounts across a variety of social media platforms. Recent research indicated that neither the children nor their parents tend to be aware that online activities can be searched and replicated and that social media posts can have negative ramifications in the future such as losing scholarships, and even suspension from education institutions (James et al., 2019). Because cyberspace knows no boundaries, internet-related sexual crime is believed to increase and diversify in coming years (Hymas, 2019). This includes online video games (Kumar et al., 2017) and sexual solicitation (Schulz et al., 2016).

In the following online risks to children will be examined. These include the concepts of *content risk* and *contact risk,* which are associated with children's online participation such as playing games and communicating with friends through social networking sites.

ONLINE RISKS TO CHILDREN

The main reason children use digital technology is for spending time with friends (Anderson & Jiang, 2018). These interactions include gaming, texting, and social media communication. In this regard, two categories of sexual online risks exist, which have been identified as *content risk* and *contact risk,* albeit they are not entirely mutually exclusive (Livingstone & Smith, 2014). *Content risk* refers to the child being the recipient of, usually adult produced, mass content such as online pornography (Australian Institute of Family Studies, 2017). By contrast, *contact risk* is related to willing or unwilling online interaction with someone else (another child or an adult).

Content Risk

Some voices have become loud indicating that online child sexual depiction in cartoons and video games are harmless because they do not involve direct contact with real children and as such there are no legal or even moral concerns (Brown & Shelling, 2019). We disagree with such reasoning. Furthermore, the lines between fantasy and reality may easily be blurred, which can be seen in the example of online gaming.

Many children engage in online gaming, which has numerous benefits. Positive effects include cognitive, emotional, motivational and specific skills development, which have been attributed to benefit online and real-life interactions (Granic, Lobel & Engels, 2014). Video games have been successfully introduced in educational curricula (Girard, Ecelle, & Magnant, 2013; Mayer, 2019) and e-homework (Dobozy, 2014) to the point where they replace conventional textbooks (Schwartz, 2014). However, there are specific dangers of online gaming, which adults need to be aware of to protect children adequately from harm. Such dangers include gaming platforms.

Roblox, a popular entertainment platform for children, is rapidly expanding globally. It allows users to develop their own multiplayer games (completely uncensored), which brings 'the world together through play' (Roblox, 2019). Perez (2019) stated that Roblox 'has become a place that kids go to 'hang out' online even then not actively playing' (n. p.). However, user-generated games are not regulated, which mean that children can easily be exposed to inappropriate sexualised and violent content. Lanier (2018) reported that a seven-year-old girl showed her mother a playground scene depicting two male avatars raping the girl's avatar. The mother was quoted as follows: 'Words cannot describe the shock, disgust and guilt that I am feeling... I was able to take screenshots of what I was witnessing so people will realize just how horrific this experience was' (Lanier, 2018, n. p.). Similarly, in Australia, a mother stated that her six-year-old daughter 'was invited to a "sex room" in Roblox that depicted a group of avatars engaging in explicit sex acts' (Dick, 2019, n. p.).

Unsuspecting parents may be unaware of the dangers associated with games available on the Roblox platform. User-to-user interactions and sharing content via online chat rooms and social media networks may result in children being at risk being taken advantage of. Consequently, it is imperative that parents use security measures to protect their children from risk of harm. However, security settings offered by Roblox do not seem effective as they can easily be overridden (Lanier, 2018). Some children have been found to use so-called third-party applications to override parental controls to communicate with other players online. In this regard, it is important that parents be aware of the 'overlay' function and recognise that more effective ways to protect children are required.

In response to publicly raised concerns, Roblox employed a security expert to develop online safety measures along with a 'digital civility program' aimed at child users to provide education in creating a safer gaming environment (Lanier, 2019). In this regard, the question arises whether children should be made responsible for their safety while participating online through video games using the Roblox entertainment platform. Given Roblox's increased globalisation efforts, public scrutiny is critically important particularly against the background of sexualised content having been created reportedly through hackers (Lanier, 2019), which is an example of how children are exposed to *content risk* while playing seemingly innocent online games.

In addition, children are exposed to sexual exploitation materials on websites (Fradd, 2017) or deliberately engage in sexual interaction with others, which appear to be the new 'normal' (Symons, Ponnet, Walrave, & Heirman, 2018). This includes 'sexting' (Collins et al., 2017; Temple & Choi, 2014). However, this is not always consensual and undertaken willingly, being free of coercion.

Contact Risk - Sexting

Children connect with new friends online through game play and social media. These online friendships develop through shared interest, which may include flirting with each other, leading to sexting behaviours (Madigan, Ly, Rash, Van Ouytsel, & Temple, 2018). The concept of 'sexting' commonly refers to consensually sending a partially nude or fully nude images or videos to specified and intended recipients. This can also include sexual text messages (Thomas, 2018). Sexting has become normalised among children (Johnson et al., 2018) and even adults (Grobbelaar & Guggisberg, 2018).

Reasons for sexting are complex and this behaviour seems to have become socially normal and accepted. Children and adolescents are motivated to engage in sexting behaviours for several reasons including being flirtatious, having fun, or to fulfil someone's requests for a 'sexy present' (Madigan & Temple, 2018). Sexting has been found to be used as a 'currency of trust' (James et al., 2019, p. 30) whereby children convey intimacy, and seek peer validation (Thomas, 2018). This may pose a specific dilemma for girls as sometimes they are pressured into providing sexual images of themselves (Englander & McCoy, 2017). In a recent study, Thomas (2018) examined stories, which revealed that boys used coercion and threats when persistent requests for a sexual image were unsuccessful. Findings indicated that even if initially girls refused to send sexts, eventually they submitted to the coercion. Thomas (2018) concluded that girls require specific skills 'to successfully navigate the challenges they face' (p. 192) in relation to coercion to send sexts.

In addition to sexts being requested by recipients, they have been found to be shared without appropriate consent (Thomas, 2018). Even though there is no gender difference in the frequency of sexting, society tends to apply different standards for girls when compared to boys (Johnson, et al., 2018). Girls experience disapproval to a greater extent than boys for sending sexts. For example, girls tend to be held responsible for sexts they send their boyfriends if the boys share these intimate pictures without the girls' consent with other boys (Johnson et al., 2018). Sharing sexts without the original sender's consent can involve either forwarding or showing a sext to at least one person or post it to a social media or photo-sharing site (James et al., 2019). In a US study of 1320 students, researchers found that those who have refused to engage in sexting are most at risk of having their pictures released without their consent. Risk factors for the unauthorised distribution of sexual images include younger age, those who are initially pressured into releasing sexts and those who engage with multiple recipients (Englander & McCoy, 2017). Therefore, children should be educated on healthy and age-appropriate online interaction and practicing refusal skills (e.g., when being pressured into providing sexual content) along with looking out for each other (James et al., 2019).

Unintended consequences of sexting may result in what has become known as 'sextortion' (Grobbelaar & Guggisberg, 2018). Through the use of bribery, threats and blackmail sexual images and/or videos are demanded of the victimised person, which is a growing problem among even young children. Sextortion is an emerging crime with law enforcement experts and researchers agreeing that it is a frequent occurrence (Witters, Poplin, Jurecic, & Spera, 2016). It is a particularly dangerous crime for children because of the shame and fear sextortion causes, which often leads to keeping the blackmail from their parents (Kopecky, 2017). Children should be educated on the problematic nature of non-consensual distribution of sexts and urged to disclose any form of coercion or blackmail. In this regard it is important to note that advocating for refraining from engaging in sexting is ineffective given the extent to which it has become common practice (Johnson et al., 2018).

With regard to the characteristics and motivation of children who share sexts without the sender's consent, further research is needed. Specific prevention strategies can only be developed after a better understanding is gained on individuals and their decision-making process to the unlawful distribution of sexts and possible other criminal behaviour. Identification of effective deterrents is urgently needed to reduce the prevalence of non-consensual sharing of sexts.

Contact Risk – Sexual Solicitation

There is an overlap between online and offline harm from cyber victimization (Schulz et al., 2016), for example, if children are groomed for sexual purposes (Livingstone et al., 2015). Ybarra and colleagues (2007) defined the concept of online sexual solicitationas behaviour that is 'encouraging someone to talk about sex, to do something sexual, or to share personal sexual information' (p. 32), which may involve impersonation.

Online sexual solicitation does not only occur by strangers but also from individuals known to the child. This includes asking for sexual information and sexual content. Research indicates that children as young as 10 years have been targeted by online sexual solicitation with estimates being higher than offline contact sexual abuse (Livingstone & Smith, 2014). Alarmingly, there is emerging evidence from the UK suggesting that children experience higher levels of online sexual victimisation by perpetrators known to them in real life rather than being groomed by a stranger online. This is important because of the misconception commonly referred to as 'stranger danger,' which predominantly focuses on unknown persons and neglects empirical evidence that suggests increased danger from known individuals.

Empirical evidence consistently suggests that parents are anxious about strangers in relation to protecting children from unwanted sexual contact not only offline but also online (James et al., 2019; Schulz et al., 2016). A European study among children found that 30% aged between nine and 16 years had contacted an unknown person online. The prevalence increased to nearly 50% among 15–16 year olds, of which about one in 10 went to meet someone they did not know and met on the internet face-to-face. This includes contacts with 'friends of friends,' which are not perceived as meeting a stranger. This indicates increasing blurred boundaries between the notions of a 'stranger' versus an 'unknown person' (Livingstone & Smith, 2014).

It is not surprising that extended 'friendship circles' pose a challenge to safety interventions when contacts are so easily made with strangers. A recent European study investigated how children were lured into online and offline encounters with strangers (Schulz et al., 2016). Findings indicated that non-sexual online interactions sometimes led to offline sexual activities and that perpetrators were surprisingly young, with even less than five years age difference between perpetrators and victims. The same study found that engaging a child in non-sexual online interactions does not constitute a criminal offence, which has been noted by the researchers as a concerning issue. Therefore, there needs to be a balance of discussing the issues of 'stranger danger' and online interactions with friends when having a conversation with children about the risk of sexual solicitation, which should include self-disclosure (e.g., oversharing of information; sexting; having boundaries with friends). Some children are at an increased risk of online sexual solicitation than others.

Research in relation to children's online risk is in its infancy, which may explain inconsistent findings along with, sometimes highly emotional, controversies (Talves & Kalmus, 2015). What has been agreed upon is that there are disproportionate dangers for children online when compared to offline risk of harm. The literature on offline vulnerability to sexual victimisation in childhood suggests that risk factors compound each other in complex ways, resulting in possible increased online risk of victimization (Livingstone, et al., 2015). This includes repeat sexual victimization of those who have a history of intrafamilial child sexual abuse (see Guggiberg, 2018), which may be an important risk factor of online sexual risk taking in adolescence. It is not surprising that children who have unrestricted online access without parental control are at greatest risk of harm including from sexual solicitation (Talves & Kalmus, 2015).

While some offenders engage in extensive grooming to establish a trusting relationship, others seek instant gratification by introducing sexual content early on in the online interaction (Schulz et al., 2016). In their study across three European countries (Finland, Germany and Sweden), Schulz and colleagues (2016) investigated sexual solicitation behaviours of over 2800 individuals. Sexual online contact included 'sexting' (i.e., sending and receiving sexual images, engaging in cyber sexual activity), and offline sexual activities. In this regard, the researchers stated that 'all participants who had met a child off-line reported engaging in off-line sexual activity with them' (p. 175). Respondents reported that they solicited adolescents and children of both sexes, with girls being targeted at a higher rate than boys. Approximately one in three participants reported to have solicited more than 20 victims with sexual outcomes. Furthermore, the study found that younger children were at a higher risk than adolescents for in-person sexual victimisation, once offenders were able to successfully engage them. The researchers concluded that even young children who use the internet may become targeted by offenders, which is why prevention efforts should address all potential victims including young girls and boys, adolescents, as well as parents and educators. This is critically important because, 'caretakers often underestimate hat children do online, while overestimating their child's knowledge of self-protective means' (Schulz et al., 2016, p. 182).

Sexual offenders seem to have unlimited opportunities to engage with potential victims online, whereby parents and/or educators as capable guardians have been found to be largely absent (de Santisteban & Gamez-Guadix, 2018). Usually, offenders solicit numerous victims at the same time. While research indicates that girls are at a higher risk of online sexual solicitation than boys (de Santisteban & Gamez-Guadix, 2018; James et al., 2019; Livingstone & Smith, 2014), some offenders specifically target boys (Schulz et al., 2016). Consequently, appropriate prevention measures should target both genders equally.

PREVENTATIVE MEASURES

Parents and educators play a critical role in helping children navigate the internet to ensure digital devices are used safely and responsibly. Parents of young and older children have expressed their concerns about online content seeking advice from schools and teachers on 'parenting in a digital age' (James et al., 2019, p. 9). This includes the time the children spend on online devices, what information they are exposed to, but also how they interact with others, and what boundaries parents should set to manage digital participation.

It is important to note that parents play an important role in modelling appropriate digital habits. Unsurprisingly, children pay attention to what their parents do. In this regard, James and colleagues (2019) argued that parents' digital habits and how they manage their own devices are powerful influences and should not be underestimated. Therefore, parents have an opportunity to influence their children's online behaviour simply by being a positive role model. Furthermore, children can develop resiliency and overcome potential dangers through having digital literacy skills (Livingstone et al., 2015).

Digital Literacy

It is imperative that children develop skills in relation to safe online participation even at a young age. Kumar and colleagues (2017) argued that education should commence at a young age to help them build 'a stronger foundation when they transition to adolescence and adulthood amid a rapidly evolving Internet landscape' (p. 16). Research indicates that digital literacy education has a beneficial effect (James et al., 2019). Consequently, children require adult guidance in developing knowledge and skills how to engage in appropriate and safe online participation. As discussed above, the value of digital technology is uncontested. However, given the online risks, valuable opportunities for adults to discuss the particular challenges posed by gaming platforms and social media interaction should not be missed.

Teaching children digital literacy skills and helping them understand cyber safety appear to be more important than ever. This includes ensuring they know how to identify and respond to digital dilemmas. Opportunities may be taken to raise children's interest and teach them how to navigate the digital world and use technology safely and responsibly. It is important to recognise that restriction and creating an atmosphere of fear are unhelpful and counterproductive. Instead, it is necessary to equip children to be digitally aware and knowledgeable about online risks; this goes beyond providing them with a list of what to do and what not to do. A prerequisite is having a productive relationship with the children. Only then is it possible to teach them to be courageous and offer them advice if necessary. Communicating that parents and their children are a team who help each other navigate the complex online space appears to be a more promising approach than utilising authoritative control and instilling fear. Children who feel supported may be more likely to reach out when they are unsure about unsafe interactions.

Other strategies include raising awareness about disclosing personal information when being online, sitting next to the children when they are online, and setting clear boundaries for using online devices. Furthermore, online information such as the links below may be explored together with the children:

- Australia–Kids Helpline https://kidshelpline.com.au/ and Alannah & Madeline Foundation https://www.digitallicence.com.au/ and Cyber Smart Kids Quiz https://www.esafety.gov.au/kids-quiz/ along with the online safety guide by the eSafety Commissioner https://www.esafety.gov.au/parents/online-safety-guide
- Canada–Kids Help Phone https://kidshelpphone.ca/
- UK–Childline https://www.childline.org.uk/
- USA–Teen line Your Life Your Voice https://teenlineonline.org/ yyp/121-help-me-2/ and http://www.yourlifeyourvoice.org/Pages/ home.aspx.

FUTURE DIRECTIONS

It is imperative to take online safety seriously rather than having 'a faith-based approach to cyber security, in that we pray every night that nothing bad will happen' (Shackelford, 2019, p. 28). Livingstone and colleagues (2015) warned that it should not be assumed that children are 'media savvy' (p. 13). As discussed above, extensive evidence suggests that many children are vulnerable to risk of harm, which requires focus on building empowerment (Mascheroni et al., 2014). This includes knowing what action to take in the event of victimization. Children should be assured that despite the risks, internet technology does have many advantages, and that with caution and open communication, the issues can be mastered together.

Research is required to gain further insight into children's internet access, often through personal devices, for gaming and social interaction purposes. Additionally, investigations should focus on parents and educators to determine their ability to monitor the children's interaction and identify protective factors that may assist the adult-child relationship to (further) develop resiliency. This includes the evaluation of prevention strategies implemented in the family home along with educational settings. Finally, empirical understanding should be increased in relation to the similarities, differences and possible compounding effects of online versus offline risks of sexual victimization.

CONCLUSION

Children and adolescents increasingly integrate mobile technologies into their daily lives. This requires parents, educators and researchers alike to understand the complex interplay between social interaction on the internet and its dangers. This chapter discussed issues important for women concerned about cyber safety for children. A brief overview was given of the rapid growth of the internet and children's access to new technologies, emphasising their right to interact in the online space, while being aware of the digital footprint. Following this, sexual risks were examined with focus on children, which included the concepts of *content risk* and *contact risk*, which are not mutually exclusive. Examples discussed included online video games, sexting and sexual solicitation. Consideration was given to digital literacy to assist children develop skills to participate safely online.

Given the increased risk of children in relation to sexting and online solicitation, prevention efforts should target girls and boys. Treating online risk seriously should not involve restricting access to devices, as such an approach seems ineffective and even counterproductive. Clearly, children deserve to participate online and discover their potentials. They need to be equipped from a young age to navigate the challenges posed by digital technologies and manage risks effectively with the guidance of parents and other adults. It is imperative that the opportunity is not missed to engage young children and teach them important online safety behaviours. Managing children's use of internet technologies is complex - it requires contextual awareness, knowledge and understanding.

REFERENCES

Anderson, M., and J. Jiang, 2018. *Teens, social media & technology.* Washington, DC: Pew Research Center. Retrieved from: https://www. pewinternet.org/2018/05/31/teens-social-media-technology-2018/.

Australian Human Rights Commission, 2019. Face the facts: Gender equality 2018. Sydney, NSW: Author. Retrieved from: https://www. humanrights.gov.au/our-work/education/face-facts-gender-equality-2018.

Australian Institute of Family Studies, 2017. The effects of pornography on children and young people: An evidence scan. Southbank, VIC: Author. Retrieved from: https://aifs.gov.au/publications/effects-pornography-children-and-young-people/part-synthesis-report.

Brown, R., and J. Shelling, 2019. Exploring the implications of child sex dolls. *Trends and Issues in Crime and Criminal Justice, 570,* 1–13. Retrieved from https://aic.gov.au/publications/tandi/tandi570.

Collins, R. L., V. C. Strasburger, J. D. Brown, E. Donnerstein, A. Lenhart, and M. Ward, 2017. Sexual media and childhood well-being and health. *Pediatrics, 140,* 162–166.

deSantisteban, P., and M. Gamez-Guadix, 2018. Prevalence and risk factors among minors for online solicitations and interactions with adults. *The Journal of Sex Research, 55*, 939–950.

Dick, S. 2019, 10 July. 'Traumatised and violated': Popular children's video game hijacked by sexual predators. *The New Daily.* Retrieved from: https://thenewdaily.com.au/life/tech/2019/07/10/roblox-cyber-safety/?utm_source=Adestra&utm_medium=email&utm_campaign=Morning%20News%20-%2020190711.

Dobozy, E. 2014. E-homework is widening the gap for disadvantaged students. *The Conversation.* Retrieved from: https://theconversation.com/e-homework-is-widening-the-gap-for-disadvantaged-students-31047.

Englander, E. K., and M. McCoy, 2017. Pressured sexting and revenge porn in a sample of Massachusetts adolescents. *International Journal of Technoethics, 8*, 16–25.

Fradd, M. 2017. *The porn myth: Exposing the reality behind the fantasy of pornography.* San Francisco, CA: Ignatius Press.

Girard, C., J. Ecalle, and A. Magnant, 2013. Serious games as new educational tools: How effective are they: A meta-analysis of recent studies. *Journal of Computer Assisted Learning, 29*, 207–219.

Granic, I., A. Lobel, and R. C. M. E. Engels, 2014. The benefits of playing video games. *American Psychologist, 69*, 66–78.

Grobbelaar, M., and M. Guggisberg, 2018. Sexually explicit images: Examining the lawful and unlawful new forms of sexual engagement. In M. Guggisberg, & J. Henricksen (eds.). *Violence against women in the 21st century: Challenges and future directions* (pp. 133–160). New York, NY: Nova Science Publishers.

Guggisberg, M. 2018. The impact of violence against women and girls: A life span analysis. In M. Guggisberg & J. Henricksen (eds.). *Violence against women in the 21st century: Challenges and future directions* (pp. 3–27). New York, NY: Nova Science Publishers.

Hymas, C. 2019, 11 February. Cyber sex crimes against children have trebles in three years NSPCC warns. London, UK: *The Telegraph.*

Retrieved from: https://www.telegraph.co.uk/news/2019/02/11/cyber-sex-crimes-against-children-have-trebled-three-years-nspcc/.

James, C., E. Weinstein, and K. Mendoza, 2019. *Teaching digital citizens in today's world: Research and insights behind the common sense K–12 digital citizenship curriculum.* San Francisco, CA: Common Sense Media. Retrieved from: https://d1e2bohyu2u2w9.cloudfront.net/education/sites/default/files/tlr_component/common_sense_education_digital_citizenship_research_backgrounder.pdf.

Johnson, M., F. Mishna, M. Okumu, and J. Daciuk, 2018. *Non-consensual sharing of sexts: Behaviours and attitudes of Canadian youth.* Ottawa, Canada: MediaSmarts.

Kopecky, K. 2017. Online blackmail of Czech children focused on so-called "sextortion" (analysis of culprit and victim behaviours). *Telematics and Informatics, 34,* 11–19.

Korioth, T. 2015. Know the emotional, physical signs of teen dating violence. *American Academy of Paediatricians.* Retrieved from: https://www.aappublications.org/content/36/4/26.6.

Kumar, P., S. M. Naik, U. R. Devkar, M. Chetty, T. L. Clegg, and J. Vitak, 2017. 'No telling pass codes out because they're private': Understanding children's mental models of privacy and security online. *Proceedings of the ACM on Human-Computer Interaction, 1,* 1–21. Retrieved from https://dl.acm.org/citation.cfm?doid=3171581.3134699.

Lanier, L. 2019, 15 January. *Roblox launches digital civility.* Los Angeles, CA: Variety Media. Retrieved from: https://variety.com/2019/gaming/news/roblox-launches-digital-civility-1203107649/.

Lanier, L. 2018, 05 July. *Video game 'Roblox' showed a 7-year-old girl's avatar being raped.* Los Angeles, CA: Variety Media. Retrieved from: https://variety.com/2018/gaming/news/roblox-little-girl-avatar-raped-1202865698/.

Livingstone, S., J. Carr, and J. Byrne, 2015. *One in three: Internet governance and children's rights.* Paper Series No. 22. London, UK: Centre for International Governance Innovation & Royal Institute of International Affairs.

Livingstone, S., and P. K. Smith, 2014. Harms experienced by child users of online and mobile technologies: The nature, prevalence and management of sexual aggressive risks in the digital age. *Journal of Child Psychology and Psychiatry, 55,* 635–654.

Madigan, S., and J. Temple, 2018, 27 February. One in seven teens are 'sexting' says new research. *The Conversation.* Retrieved from: https://theconversation.com/one-in-seven-teens-are-sexting-says-new-research-92170.

Madigan, S., A. Ly, C. L. Rash, J. Van Ouytsel, and J. R. Temple, 2018. Prevalence of multiple forms of sexting behavior among youth: A systematic review and meta-analysis. *JAMA Pediatrics, 172,* 327–335.

Mascheroni, G., A. Jorge, and L. Farrugia, 2014. Media representations and children's discourses on online risks: Findings from qualitative research in nine European countries. *Cyberpsychology: Journal of Psychosocial Research on Cyberspace, 8,* 1 - 18. Retrieved from: http://dx.doi.org/10.5817/CP2014-2-2.

Mayer, R. E. 2019. Computer games in education. *Annual Review of Psychology, 70,* 531–549.

Peter, I. 2004. So, who really did invent the internet? *Net History.* Retrieved from: http://www.nethistory.info/History%20of%20the%20Internet/origins.html.

Perez, S. 2019, 08 April. Roblox hits milestone of 90 million monthly active users. *TechCrunch*, Verizon Media. Retrieved from: https://techcrunch.com/2019/04/08/roblox-hits-milestone-of-90m-monthly-active-users/.

Roblox. 2019. Powering imagination. Retrieved from: https://www.roblox.com/?v=rc&rbx_source=3&rbx_medium=cpa&rbx_campaign=1628715797.

Schulz, A., E. Bergen, P. Schuhmann, J. Hoyer, and P. Santtila, 2016. Online sexual solicitation of minors: How often and between whom does it occur? *Journal of Research in Crime and Delinquency, 53,* 165–188.

Schwartz, K. 2014. Bypassing the textbook: Video games transform social studies curriculum. Retrieved from https://www.kqed.org/

mindshift/33243/forget-the-textbook-video-games-as-social-studies-content.

Shackelford, S. J. 2019. Should cybersecurity be a human right? Exploring the 'shared responsibility' of cyber peace. *Stanford Journal of International Law,* 17–55.

Smith, R. G., and P. N. Grabosky, 2012. Cyber crime. In M. Marmo, W. De Lint, and D. Palmer (eds.). *Crime and justice: A guide to criminology* (4th ed., pp. 245–274). Pyrmont, NSW: Thomson Reuters.

Symons, K., K. Ponnet, M. Walrave, and W. Heirman, 2018. Sexting scripts in adolescent relationships: Is sexting becoming the norm? *New Media & Society, 20,* 3836–3857.

Talves, K., and V. Kalmus, 2015. Gendered mediation of children's internet use: A keyhole for looking into changing socialization practices. *Cyberpsychology: Journal of Psychosocial Research on Cyberspace, 9,* 1–18; article 4. doi: 10.5817/CP2015-1-4.

Temple, J. R., and H. J. Choi 2014. Longitudinal association between teen sexting and sexual behaviour. *Paediatrics, 134,* 1–6.

Thomas, S. E. 2018. "What should I do?": Young women's reported dilemmas with nude photographs. *Sexuality Research and Social Policy, 15,* 192–207.

Wittes, B., C. Poplin, Q., Jurecic, and C. Spera, 2016. Sextortion: Cybersecurity, teenagers, and remote sexual assault. *Centre for Technology Innovations at Brookings.* Retrieved from https://www.brookings.edu/research/sextortion-cybersecurity-teenagers-and-remote-sexual-assault/.

Ybarra, M. L., D. L. Espelage, and K. J. Mitchell, 2007. The co-occurrence of internet harassment and unwanted sexual solicitation victimization and perpetration: Associations with psychosocial indicators. *Journal of Adolescent Health, 41,* 31–41.

In: Advances in Sociology Research
Editor: Jared A. Jaworski

ISBN: 978-1-53616-781-8
© 2020 Nova Science Publishers, Inc.

Chapter 6

SEX APPEAL: NUDITY AND SEXUAL INNUENDOS IN CONTEMPORARY TEEN MAGAZINES

Umana Anjalin[1,] and Abhijit Mazumdar[2]*

[1]University of Tennessee, Knoxville, US
[2]Park University, Missouri, US

ABSTRACT

Teenage magazine advertisement portrayals of women are disputable due to the potential of these ads to acculturate women in stereotypical ways. These ads also are a cause for concern for teenage magazine readers. Adolescents or teenagers lacking social and mental maturity could be vulnerable to such exploitation that use pornographic content in advertisements. Following the examination of trends in contemporary female teenage magazines, this chapter is going to illustrate how a greater part of female models are being shown in agreeable, subordinate and sexualized ways using nude, half-clad appearances of men and women. These models are shown in overtly sexual dispositions, as well as using of sensual suggestions with sexual suggestiveness or innuendos with the placement of sexual cues in these ads. The unrealistic image portrayals in

*Corresponding Author's Email: anjalin.umana@gmail.com; uanjalin@vols.utk.edu.

these advertisements could be` inherently dangerous. Overall, the outcomes raise causes for concern over the potential effect of magazine advertisements on adolescents and young ladies' self-image and welfare.

Keywords: advertisement, teenage magazines, stereotype, sexuality, nudity, adolescence

INTRODUCTION

The contemporary teen magazine advertisements, especially in the USA, are rife with body display and erotically stimulating advertising. Women are often depicted as mere sexual objects with no functional purpose in the advertisements. Despite negative consumer attitudes and lower brand recall, ironically, these ads are often placed even when targeting the women (LaTour and Henthorne, 1993; LaTour, 1990; Nelson and Paek, 2005; Severn, Belch, and Belch, 1990). Let alone the availability of myriad kinds of sexual contents in the regular media; the teen magazines are no different when it comes to the pervasiveness of sexualized media content, and covert and overt references to sex. Adolescents indeed reside in a sexual media world, and the more of these content they see, the more they will be sexually active (Pardun, L'Engle, and Brown, 2005). For early adolescents, once they start to get acquainted with their new sexual milieu, they are on the lookout for new information on dating and sexual relationships. With time as they reach maturity, they recognize their choice of sexual content they will be more interested in — whether sexual health messages, relationships, or may be contents based on partial nudity (Pardun, L'Engle, and Brown, 2005).

Adolescence is the time of turning point, especially when it comes to sexuality as teens move towards the development of sexual identities and attitude consciousness. The transition period is marked with the ocean of mediated texts and the influence of popular culture (Durham, 1998). Adolescents' nowadays have easy access to sexual media content (SMC) of varying degrees and explicitness. This has important consequences. According to (Brown, 2009; Ward, 2003), traditional media like TV and magazines increasingly feature sexual content. Zillman (2000) argues that easy availability/access to increasing SMC may have negative consequences.

Goffman's classic study of magazine content analysis depicted gender roles during the 1970s that demonstrated that women were portrayed in the roles of mothers, sometimes as non-serious like children, or perhaps only as sex objects (Goffman: 1979). Those were the traditional portrayals of women. It was, therefore, necessary to investigate how women were portrayed in contemporary magazines, especially those directed to teenage women. The magazines directed to adolescent female consumers orient the audience with the explicit and implicit messages of adolescent socio-economic lifestyle.

The concerns are based on three assumptions. 1) Content analyses reveal that representation of sex and sexuality in SMC is not realistic (Brown, 2009; Ward, 2003); 2) Adolescents lack the emotional and social maturity as well as sexual experience to put SMC, notably pornographic content into perspective (Thornburgh and Lin, 2002); 3) Along with peers, SMC has outperformed parents and schools as a source of sexual information (Kaiser Family Foundation, 2003).

Other scholars, on the other hand, have argued that sex should not be seen as inherently dangerous, and adolescents should not be regarded as necessarily vulnerable to SMC (Attwood & Smith, 2011). Rather, adolescents' use of SMC should be studied within an emphasis on their critical skills and active appropriation of the content (Lerum and Dworkin, 2009). MGQore frequent reading of mainstream magazines (e.g., *Marie Claire* and *GQ*) was positively linked to young adults' knowledge about sexual health (Walsh and Ward, 2010).

Despite having the interaction of youth culture and the popular culture, studies on the analysis of adolescence, culture, mass media, and sexuality is scarce. According to (Valkenburg and Peter, 2013) study, regarding the scholarly discussion about media and adolescents' sexual development, little research can be found; and if so, it is scattered and not cumulative. Regarding media and sexual cognition, overall the studies have shown that when young people use SMC more often, they strongly believe that sex without relational commitment is acceptable and are likely to hold more permissive beliefs about sex (Ward and Friedman, 2006; Brown & L'Engle, 2009). This chapter will try to focus on gendered ideologies of sexuality, exposure types media content, risk factors, usage examples of sexual advertisements, cultural trends, and future implications.

DIFFERENT TYPES OF EXPOSURE

There is a strong positive association between exposure to exclusive media content of sexual nature and intentional sexual acts (Pardoun, L'Engle, Brown, 2005). These include different media vehicles like television shows, movies, music, magazines, internet sites, and newspapers that may sometimes contain gross sexual contents. Sometimes many these convey references to sexual intercourse and overt descriptions that contain full/partial nudity, touch and kiss, sexual relationships and innuendos, sexual intercourse, pubertal issues, etc. (Pardun, L'Engle, Brown, 2005; Nelson and Paek, 2005). Here print advertising, communicating through verbal and visual imagery often depict sexualized elements (Soley and Kurzbard, 1986). The more any adolescent or teen sees sexual media content, the more he or she will be included to be sexually active and/or anticipate greater sexual activities (Pardun, L'Engle, Brown, 2005).

Usage of sex appeal is an approach marketers often use to build brand awareness. For quite some time, five ways sexuality has been employed in advertising:

1. Subliminal techniques (use of sexual cues in advertisements that affect the audience's subconscious mind).
2. The sensuality that the women who might respond to which is more of a sensual suggestion than a blatant sexual approach (For example, in place of placing a strong sexual image, a tempting glance across a crowded room is depicted).
3. Sexual suggestiveness, in making the product seem more appealing.

4. Nudity or partial nudity (Piron and Young, 1996; Pope, Voges, Mark, and Brown, 2004), depicting both the genders
5. Explicit sexuality, which is more common nowadays.

The advertising contents, mainly the copy and visuals, overtly relating to sex and sexuality, conform to Goffman's (1979) gendered ideologies in contemporary US advertisements. These represent sexualized identities of women as sexual objects of male counterparts, emphasis of female vulnerability with nudity and provocative postures, sexual explicitness with the exposure of girls' bosom, derriere, bodily curvature, and genitals, feminine self-touching of themselves, body positions related to sexual submission to men, and facial gestures implying coyness, sexual or eroticized ecstasy, and coyness (Anjalin, 2015; Durham, 1998).

FACTORS LEADING TO EXPOSURE

There are many risk factors that contribute to harm regarding pornography exposure, including demographical factors like age, gender, personal characteristics, attitude, and social contexts like peers, society, family, or culture. The nature of pornographic exposure may be inadvertent (unintentional/unsolicited) or intentional (deliberate). These include contents of sexual nature that range from nudity to open sexual activities that may contain violence of immoderate features (sexual explicitness) having potentially negative outcomes (Bryant, 2010).

More males than females are not only exposed to pornographic contents like inadvertent online exposure, or X-rated contents but also will seek out these sexually explicit materials (deliberate exposure) and make more consumption of these at a greater rate than their female counterparts (Bryant, 2010; Flood and Hamilton, 2003). All these inadvertent or intentional exposure vary by age, gender, and biological factors (Wallmyr and Welin, 2006). Males also differ than females in their preference in engaging with pornographic media. Demographic factors like age, especially during adolescence and emerging adulthood also mirrors the biological and cognitive cycle that transforms desire, interest, and level of risk-taking that increases with age (Carroll, Padilla-Walker, Nelson, Olson, McMamara, Barry, and Madsen, 2008; Ybarra and Mitchell, 2005). Here, curiosity motivated factors also remain a crucial aspect, especially with females (Wallmyr and Welin, 2006). Gender differences in the acceptance of pornography, reasons for use, and sexual socialization can be observed in the social context of exposure as well. Young males tend to have more exposure when in the presence of their friends (Wolak, Mitchell, and Finkelhor, 2007), while females watch more of these contents more often with their partners (Wallmyr and Welin, 2006). Personal characteristics, to some extent, play a central role in pornography use, too. Although the use of pornography remained a taboo for quite some time, and consequently, there is a robust association between the 'risk-taking'/'rule-breaking' behaviors and the use of pornographic content. High rates of deliberate exposure and enactment of rule-breaking behaviors are thus common, especially among the delinquent youth, even younger adolescents under the age of 10 and sensation-seeking individuals (Bjørnbekk, 2003; Peter and Valkenburg, 2006; Wolak, Mitchell, and Finkelhor, 2007).

SELLING OF SEX FANTASY: THE RECENT TYPES OF EXPOSURE EXAMPLES

It is un-mistakenly evident that sex sells and the connection between fashion and sex is nothing new. The fashionable women of yesterdays have been habituated appearing in décolleté attires in thinner-most fabrics. Many ads in the contemporary teen magazines, particularly the ones that promote perfumes and cosmetics, for example, Viva Glam, KARL LARGERFELD, SIMON Malls, PRADA Candy, Calvin Klein, Chance CHANEL EauTendre, GUCCI Guilty, Viva La Juicy — Juicy Couture, M.A.C., Herbal Essences Naked, and GUESS ads have been taking advantage of sex appeals when trying to cut through the clutter. These advertisements portray women being fully naked or half-clad in backless clothes while having exposed mostly their skin, cleavage, navel, while being in provocatively intimate positions with their model partners (Anjalin, 2015).

By and large, the utilization of sex to make items all the more engaging is an authentic strategy for some companies, items, and marketing firms. A shock technique with mild erotic stimuli was very much prevalent in cutting through the clutter of advertisements in teen magazines. The objective ought to be to utilize sex in a way that is fascinating, fitting to the item, and within the moral measures of the region. Regardless of whether there is a transgression of a social or cultural taboo, is liable to further investigation with an examination of shopper reactions to such incitement or provocation.

TRENDS ACROSS CULTURES

The portrayal of women today has transformed them into 'sex objects' for enjoyment, especially in media. Since a lot of learning and socialization can be attributed to the print magazines, the vicariously learned 'beauty' standards can reinforce stereotypical attitudes. A relatively recent study (Zurbriggen & Morgan, 2006) found a positive correlation between magazine consumption and the conviction that sexualized beauty standards should be achieved. There have been recommended guidelines for advertising portrayals pertaining to the existing standards of social responsibility, propriety, and modesty put forward by the International Chamber of Commerce (1997). Following the guidelines of self-regulation to what is of good taste and modesty, averting to what may be objectification of women or treatment of women as decorative models, or avoiding usage of sexual imagery, sexual suggestiveness, or gender-role stereotypes and violence, some self-regulatory agencies have revamped their own rules of representations in advertising (Boddewyn, 1991; Galloni, 2001; Mueller, 2004). Nonetheless, based on different standards of modesty, taste, and values based on culture and societal norms, these standards differ and are constantly varying (Boddewyn, 1991; Mueller, 2004).

This phenomenon is not new --- the selling of clothes during the 1980s, having Brooke Shields in a tight pair of jeans or sending out a 116-page supplement in the Vanity Fair magazine in October of 1991 issue featuring near-naked men and women in provocative poses had Calvin Klein jeans have an increase of 30% in Bloomingdale sales. While nudity has been used in selling clothes, the perfume adverts have used a different tactic. The clever word-play of using the shock-tactic could be solved in a trice. As designed via the brand name, the French Connection UK brand had done with a four-letter wordplay regarding their brand FCUK is a case in point. A content analysis of 2014 advertisements of U.S. teen magazine revealed that Goffman's (1979) category of 'Body Display' included those images where the models were shown wearing provocative and skimpy clothes and lingerie; being nude (implicitly or explicitly), displaying either their intimate parts of the body or were seen wearing see-through clothing (Anjalin, 2015). Not only in USA, clothing chain store Gilly Hicks, in Sydney, Australia owned by Abercombie & Fitch, pepped up its marketing campaign with the advertising pitch pandering to adolescent sexuality. The ad used sex appeal by portraying a topless WASP mermaid and an undergarment-free beach lad, and this was a tart-up to play with selling sexual-fantasy to the high-school going students (Garfield, 2008). During 1971, Yves Saint Laurent posed as nude with only a pair of spectacles to promote his perfumes. Lacoste followed this trend having muscular men fully naked drinking coffee while sitting on an armchair. In the USA, the pre-Christmas 2003 issue of Abercombie and Fitch catalog featured group sexual acts of attractive men and women. Not only did parents with young children feel extremely offended, but also the youth were dismayed at the brands' brazen attempt to manipulate them (The Economist, 2004).

The use of sexual cues in advertising is a result of multiple factors. A study of content analysis of print advertising towards young women audience in seven countries — Brazil, China, France, India, Korea, Thailand, and the USA attested to this fact (Nelson and Paek, 2005). From the analysis, the researchers concluded that everything related to contextual factors that derive from personal values regarding sexual liberty, masculinity cultural values, and political-economic framework severely affect the levels of nudity portrayed in advertising. For example, in Westernized cultures, nondomestic models were expected to be depicted sexually than domestic models. Chinese advertisements, on the other hand, showed a lesser degree of sexuality than the other countries had shown, possibly due to the restrictive reason of political-economic system of Communism there. The editorial content, therefore, abided by tight control, which resulted in fewer sexually explicit images in Chinese magazines. On the other hand, the Thai and French ads depicted the highest level of sexuality in this matter. Thailand, being an Asian country, had a strict political system and having highly religious people, the scenario was somewhat unexpected. However, looking at the religion most Thailand dwellers follow, it became obvious that Buddhism, the primary religion followed there is less restrictive on predisposition about sex than the orthodox Judeo-Christian sects. Buddhism also has a place for prostitutes in religion (Hofstede, 1998). Prostitutes are not stigmatized in Thailand as they are in Western countries (Kirsch, 1985). However, advertising examples having the same values and tastes of sexual content as of Thailand should not be compared with that of other Asian countries. There, of course, are multiple factors that may be responsible for such execution in Thailand (Nelson and Paek, 2005). French advertising is a stark contrast to most Asian country advertisements. Ads featured in the Indian women's magazines also conform somewhat to the portrayal of a higher level of sexuality by nondomestic models (Karan, 2003).

HARMS OF EXPOSURE

A key criticism of sexually-based advertising is that it continues to maintain dissatisfaction with one's body. The highly idealized body types like 'curvaceously thin' (in the case of women) or 'muscularly lean' (in the case of men) portrayed in the media (Flynn, Park, Morin, Stana, 2015) could be a source of body dissatisfaction. If the body dissatisfaction is internalized, teenagers, especially teenage women, would place physical attractiveness as one of their crucial values. Nubile young women such as young starlets would be most likely to camouflage their histrionic shortcomings with the alternative of surgically enhanced options (Hulse, 2000). The girls pay a hefty price living in an overly sexualized culture (Liebau, 2007). Ads that portray women as sex objects cause increased body dissatisfaction among women (Lavine, Sweeney, and Wagner, 1999; Graff, Murnen, and Krause, 2013; Ghaznavi and Taylor, 2015). The problem with the 'sexploitation' of the female body is that it causes a sense of inadequacy in many women. The sexual depiction of women in contemporary magazines in the USA is quite dominant in the visuals of such ads; mostly, these ad images had half-clad or fully nude women. If these messages of sexual desirability are internalized, these may ultimately become a hurdle in the way of objective self-evaluation of women in the arena of success, achievement, and future potential. Seeing models in ads in alluring and enticing positions, not only women but also men get considerably disturbed with the dissatisfaction that occurs with their erotic fantasies (Berger, 2011).

The young are inundated with exposure of unsolicited and solicited, and even violent sexual information before they can be capable enough to deal with it constructively. This effect may cause harm in changing sexual temperament and behaviors, sometimes intimate relationships and even sexuality. The early sexual activities can interfere with normal sexual development, make them habituated with 'open' sexual lifestyles like having multiple partners, casual and extramarital sex, which may not be considered appropriate in their social settings and their community. Let alone physical wellbeing; this may also make them undermine psychological and emotional wellbeing (Byant, 2010). Research also talks about the undermining of relationships and fostering of violence (Jensen and Okrina, 2004; Zillmann, 2000).

Widespread partial nudity and many times, full nudity is prevalent in media representations (Flynn, Park, Morin, and Stana, 2015) which also is evident in most of the contemporary teenage magazines. Indeed, even the minors are every day confronted with so many disturbing commercials, which are once in a while questionable. A ton of new, particularly web-based advertising commercials has emerged during the last years. In this respect, the advancement of teenagers' moral advertising literacy is essential.

CONCLUSION

According to 2014 statistics, about 3.9 million teens subscribed to the *Seventeen* Magazine and *Teen Vogue* magazine had approximately 1 million subscriptions (combining subscription and single-copy sales) and both the magazines had 93% female and 7% male subscribers (Anjalin, 2015). The way women that were depicted through the visuals of the contemporary advertisements in the teen magazines conforms to the notion that women's body could be exploited by the advertisers to move the products off the shelves. Utilization of celebrities' referent power in the promotions utilizing ridiculous showcase of the body mostly in provocative positions could be a lethal mix of the media, publicizing and celebrity culture producing typecast of what ladies should resemble, and act like. This impacts body perfect images that probably will not be physically feasible, unleashing ruin on female confidence as the audiences don't understand that the celebrities and Victoria's Secret models ought not to be worshiped,s and ladies ought not harp on unattainable outwardly engaging characteristics regularly depicted by the models who experience a livelihood of selling items by wearing them.

Here the question, however, still remains whether sex appeals are effective? Various studies have researched sex appeals and nudity in marketing goods and services. Practically every one of them presumes that sex and nudity do increase interest, paying little mind to the sexual orientation of people in the promotion or the gender of the audience. Albeit explicitly, sexually-oriented advertisements pull into consideration. However, Brand recall review for promotions utilizing sex advance is lower than promotions utilizing some other sort of appeal (Lull, Bushman, and Albarracin, 2015; Mahdawi, 2015).

Scholars have emphasized repeatedly that sexual information in media still has to become more diverse and realistic before it can serve as a trustworthy source for adolescents (Brown and Keller, 2000). Adolescents' acquisition of media literacy skills is needed to be able to evaluate the credibility and trustworthiness of sexual information in media more competently (Subrahmanyam & Smahel, 2011).

A toning down of explicit and implicit messages that uphold the notion that the road to happiness is attracting the opposite sex in the way of physical beautification is the need of the hour. The less is the touting of the value of success through allurement, appeal and seduction, the lesser would be the dissonance relating to body image and self-esteem, and lesser feelings of shame relating to appearance. If there is lesser objectification of women, the lesser would be the likelihood of alarmingly dangerous tendency of more widespread problems like sexual coercion.

REFERENCES

Anjalin, Umana. (2015). "A Content Analysis of Gender Stereotypes in Contemporary Teenage Magazines." Master's Thesis, University of Tennessee, USA. Retrieved from https://trace.tennessee.edu/utk_gra dthes/3343.

Attwood, F. & Smith, C. (2011). "Investigating young people's sexual cultures: An introduction." *Sex Education, 11*, 235-242.

Berger, A. (2011). *Ads, fads, and consumer culture: Advertising's impact on American character and society.* Lanham: Rowman & Littlefield.

Bjørnebekk.(2003).*Accessibility of violent pornography on the Internet: Revisiting a study of accessibility — prevalence and effects*, viewed May 2008, <http://www.nikk.uio.no/arrangementer/konferens/tallin03/ bjornebekk.pdf>.

Boddewyn, J. J. (1991). "Controlling sex and decency in advertising around the world."*Journal of Advertising,20*(4), 25–35.

Brown, J. & Keller, S. (2000). "Can the mass media be healthy sex educators?"*Family Planning Perspectives, 32*, 255-256.

Brown, J. & L'Engle, K. L. (2009). "X-Rated: Sexual attitudes and behaviors associated with US early adolescents' exposure to sexually explicit media."*Communication Research, 36*(1), 129-151.

Brown, J., L'Engle, K., Pardun, C., Guo, G., Kenneavy, K. & Jackson, C. (2006). "Sexy media matter: Exposure to sexual content in music, movies, television, and magazines predicts black and white adolescents' sexual behavior."*Pediatrics, 117*, 1018-27.

Bryant, C. (2010). "Adolescence, pornography and harm."*Youth Studies Australia, 29*(1), 18-26.

Bushman, B. (2007). "That was a great commercial, but what were they selling? Effects of violence and sex on memory for products in television commercials."*Journal of Applied Social Psychology, 37*, 1784–1796. doi:10.1111/j.1559-1816.2007.00237.

Carroll, J.S., Padilla-Walker, L.M., Nelson, L.J., Olson, C.D., McNamara Barry, C. & Madsen, S.D. (2008). "Generation XXX: Pornography acceptance and use among emerging adults."*Journal of Adolescent Research, 23*(1), 6-30.

Durham, M. G. (1998). "Dilemmas of desire: Representations of adolescent sexuality in two teen magazines."*Youth & Society, 29* (3), 369-389.

Flood, M. & Hamilton, C. (2003). "Youth and pornography in Australia: Evidence on the extent of exposure and likely effects." *Discussion Paper,52*, The Australia Institute, Canberra.

Flynn, M., Park, S., Morin, D. & Stana, A. (2015). "Anything but real: Body idealization and objectification of MTV docusoap characters." *Sex Roles, 72*(5), 173-182.

Galloni, A. (2001, October 25). Clampdown on "porno-chic" ads is pushed by French authorities. *Wall Street Journal*, p. B4.

Garfield, B. (2008). Abercrombie underwear shop plays up goods, but not its own. *Advertising Age,79*(10), 25. Retrieved from http://proxy.lib. utk.edu:90/login?url=http://search.ebscohost.com/login.aspx?direct=tr ue&db=ulh&AN=31244049&scope=site.

Ghaznavi, Jannath.& Taylor, Laramie D. (2015). "Bones, body parts, and sex appeal: An analysis of #thinspiration images on popular social media." *Body Image, 14,* 54.

Graff, K., Murnen, A. & Krause, S. (2013). "Low-Cut shirts and high-heeled shoes: Increased sexualization across time in magazine depictions of girls. *Sex Roles, 69,* 571-582.

Goffman, E. (1979). Gender advertisements. New York: Harper & Row.

Hofstede, G. (1998). *Masculinity and femininity: The taboo dimensionof national cultures.* Thousand Oaks, CA: Sage.

Hulse, E. (2000, September 25). Mistress Frankenstein. *Video Business, 20*(39), 14. Retrieved from http://link.galegroup.com.proxy.lib.utk.ed u:90/apps/doc/A65953764/ITOF?u=tel_a_utl&sid=ITOF&xid=5a0b85 f9.

International Chamber of Commerce. (1997). *ICC International code of advertising practice.* Retrieved March 7, 2005, from http://www.ic cwbo.org/home/statementsrules/rules/1997/advercod.asp.

Jensen, R. & Okrina, D. (2004). *"Pornography and sexual violence."* VAWnet: The National Online Resource Center on Violence Against Women, USA.

Kaiser Family Foundation. (2003). *National survey of teens and young adults on sexual health and public education campaigns: Toplines.* Menlo Park, CA: Kaiser Family Foundation.

Karan, K. (2003, May). *Advertising and the visual portrayal of the modern Indian "stereotypes."*Paper presented at the annual meeting of the International Communication Association, San Diego, CA.

Kirsch, A. T. (1985). "Buddhist sex roles/culture of gender revisited."*American Ethnologist,12,*302–320.

LaTour, M. S. (1990). "Female nudity in print advertising: An analysis of gender differences in arousal and ad response." *Psychology and Marketing, 7*(1), 65–81.

LaTour, M. S. & Henthorne, T. L. (1993). "Ethical judgements of sexual appeals in print advertising." *Journal of Advertising,23*(3), 81–90.

Liebau, C. P. (2007). *Prude: How the sex obsessed culture damages girls (and America, too!).* Boston, MA: Center Street Publishing.

Lerum, K. & Dworkin, S. L. (2009). "Bad girls rule": An interdisciplinary feminist commentary on the Report of the APA Task Force on the Sexualization of Girls."*The Journal of Sex Research, 46,* 250-63.

Lavine, H., Sweeney, D. & Wagner, S. H. (1999). Depicting women as sex objects in television advertising: Effects on body dissatisfaction. *Personality & Social Psychology Bulletin, 25,* 1049.

Lull, R., Bushman, B. & Albarracín, Dolores. (2015). "Do sex and violence sell? A meta-analytic review of the effects of sexual and violent media and ad content on memory, attitudes, and buying intentions." *Psychological Bulletin, 14,* 1022-1048.

Mahdawi, A. (2015, July 23). Sex doesn't sell -- and you'd be surprised what does; Advertisers need not despair at the news that ads with sexual content aren't effective. Habits, gorillas and brussels sprouts may all be good substitutes. Theguardian.com, p. Theguardian.com, July 23, 2015.

Mueller, B. (2004). *Dynamics of international advertising: Theoretical and practical perspectives.* New York: Peter Lang.

Nelson, M. & Paek, R. (2005). "Cross-cultural differences in sexual advertising content in a transnational women's magazine."*Sex Roles, 53*(5), 371-83.

Peter, J. & Valkenburg, P.M. (2006). Adolescents' exposure to sexually explicit online material and recreational attitudes toward sex. *Journal of Communication,56*(4), 639-60.

Valkenburg, P.M. & Peter, J. (2013). The differential susceptibility of media effects model. *Journal of Communication,63*(2), 221-243.

Pardun, C. J., L'Engle, K. L. & Brown, J. D. (2005). "Linking exposure to outcomes: Early adolescents' consumption of sexual content in six media." *Mass Communication and Society, 8*(2), 75-91.

Piron, F. & Young, M. (1996). "Consumer advertising in Germany and the United States: A study of sexual explicitness and cross-gender contact," in Global Perspectives in Cross-Cultural and Cross-National Consumer Research, Lalita A. Manrai and A jay K. Manrai, eds., New York: Haworth Press.

Pope, N. K. L., Voges, K. E., Mark, R. &Brown, M. R. (2004). "The effect of provocation in the form of mild erotica on attitude to the ad and corporate image: Differences between cause-related and product-based advertising."*Journal of Advertising,33*, 69-82.

Severn, J., Belch, G. E. & Belch, M. A. (1990). The effects of sexual and non-sexual advertising appeals and information level on cognitive processing and communication effectiveness. *Journal of Advertising, 19*, 14-22.

Soley, L. C. & Kurzbard, G. (1986). "Sex in advertising: A comparison of 1964 and 1984 magazine advertisements."*Journal of Advertising, 15*, 46–54.

Subrahmanyam, K. & Smahel, D. (2011). *Digital Youth* (Advancing Responsible Adolescent Development). New York, NY: Springer New York.

Thornburgh, D. (2002). National Research Council. Computer Science Telecommunications Board. Committee to Study Tools Strategies for Protecting Kids from Pornography Their Applicability to Other Inappropriate Internet Content, Lin, Herbert, & Ebrary, Inc. *Youth, Pornography and the Internet.*

The Economist. (2004, March 6). *Selling dreams., 370*(8365). Retrieved from http://link.galegroup.com.proxy.lib.utk.edu:90/apps/doc/A113973766/AONE?u=tel_a_utl&sid=AONE&xid=59c239c0.

Thornburgh, D. & Lin, H. (eds). (2002). *Youth, Pornography, and the Internet.* National Academy Press: Washington, DC.

Walsh, J. & Ward, L. (2010). "Magazine reading and involvement and young adults' sexual health knowledge, efficacy, and behaviors."*Journal of Sex Research,47*, 285-300.

Wallmyr, G. & Welin, C. (2006). "Young people, pornography, and sexuality: Sources and attitudes."*Journal of School Nursing,22*(5), 290-95.

Ward, L. (2002). "Does Television exposure affect emerging adults' attitudes and assumptions about sexual relationships? Correlational and experimental confirmation."*Journal of Youth and Adolescence, 31*, 1-15.

Ward, L. (2003). "Understanding the role of entertainment media in the sexual socialization of American youth: A review of empirical research."*Developmental Review, 23*, 347–388.

Ward, L. M. & Friedman, K. (2006). "Using TV as a guide: Associations between Television viewing and adolescents' sexual attitudes and behavior." *Journal of Research on Adolescence, 16*(1), 133-56.

Wolak, J., Mitchell, K. & Finkelhor, D. (2007). "Unwanted and wanted exposure to online pornography in a national sample of young internet users."*Pediatrics,119*(2), 247-57.

Ybarra, M. L. & Mitchell, K. J. (2005). "Exposure to internet pornography among children and adolescents: A national survey." *Cyberpsychology and Behavior,8*(5), 473-86.

Zillmann, D. (2000). "Influence of unrestrained access to erotica on adolescents' and young adults' dispositions toward sexuality."*Journal of Adolescent Health, 27*, 41-44.

Zurbriggen, E. L. & Morgan, E. M. (2006). "Who wants to marry a millionaire? Reality dating television programs, attitudes toward sex, and sexual behaviors."*Sex Roles, 54*, 1-17.

BIOGRAPHICAL SKETCH

Name: Umana Anjalin

Affiliation: Doctoral Candidate, College of Communication and Information, the University of Tennessee, Knoxville, Tennessee, USA

Assistant Professor (on study leave), University of Asia Pacific, Dhaka, Bangladesh

Education: Doctoral Candidate, College of Communication & Information, the University of Tennessee; M.S. in Communication & Information from University of Tennessee

Research and Professional Experience: I teach social media course at the University of Tennessee, Knoxville. I have also taught at the University of Asia Pacific in Dhaka, Bangladesh. I have industry experience in sales, marketing, and public relations experience from Bangladesh.

Professional Appointments: I have worked as an Assistant Professor, Department of Business Administration, University of Asia Pacific, Dhaka, Bangladesh. I have worked as a Research Associate in the School of Advertising and Public Relations, University of Tennessee, USA.

Honors:

- Edward J. Meeman Scholarship for Fall 2017 in CCI Honors Convocation on April 2017, from the University of Tennessee, Knoxville.
- CCI Sally J. McMillan Scholarship for the year 2016-2017 Aid Year in CCI Honors Convocation on April 11, 2016, from the University of Tennessee, Knoxville.
- CCI Karl & Madira Bickel Scholarship for the 2015-2016 Aid Year in August 2015 from the University of Tennessee, Knoxville.
- CCI Smith Graduate Scholarship (David Lee & Tina Smith Scholarship) for 2014-2015 Aid Year in April 2014 from the University of Tennessee, Knoxville.
- CCI James Fly Scholarship for the 2012-2013 Aid Year in May 2012 from University of Tennessee

Publications from the Last 3 Years:

Anjalin, Umana. & Luther, Catherine. (2018). Social Media Activism in Bangladesh: Understanding the #JusticeForTonu Movement from a Feminist Standpoint Theoretical Framework. Summer Annual AEJMC (Association for Education in Journalism, and Mass Communication) Conference 2018, August 6-9, 2018 Washington, DC, USA, organized by AEJMC.

Anjalin, Umana., Mazumdar, Abhijit.& Whiteside, Erin. (2017). 'Asian Students' Experience of Culture Shock and Coping Strategies' (ID: E173238). 2017 IBII International Conference ICBCE '17 (International Conference on Business Intelligence, Computer Science, and Education) — (for the ICESD'17 — International Conference on Education and Social Development Houston Conference). April 7-9, 2017, organized by Sam Houston State University, Houston, TX, USA.

Anjalin, Umana. & Sohel-Uz-Zaman, A. S. M. (2016). 'An Organization of Theories According to a Causal Chain Framework in Relation to Social Media Constructs for Future Research'. *2016 International Conference on Information Science, Technology, Management, Humanities & Business (ITMAHUB)*, November 21-23, 2016, organized by Malaysia Technical Scientist Association. Paper ID: #1570315891.

Sohel-Uz-Zaman, A.S. M.& Anjalin, Umana. (2016). 'Aligning Human Capital Management with Business Strategy: Strategic Human Resource Management Approach'. 2016 International Conference on Information Science, Technology, Management, Humanities & Business (ITMAHUB) November 21-23, 2016, organized by Malaysia Technical Scientist Association. Paper ID: #1570315184.

Anjalin, Umana., Mazumdar, Abhijit.& Whiteside, Erin. (2017). Asian Students' Experience of Culture Shock and Coping Strategies. *Journal of Education and Social Development*, 2017, 1–1 Sept. 2017, pages 7-13 doi: 10.5281/zenodo.834930 http://www.ibii-us.org/Journals/JESD/ ISBN 2572-9829 (Online), 2572-9810 (Print).

Name: Abhijit Mazumdar

Affiliation: Assistant professor of journalism, Park University, Missouri, USA

Education: Ph.D. in communication & information from the University of Tennessee

Research and Professional Experience: I teach journalism courses at Park University. I have also taught at the University of Tennessee. I have many years of journalism experience from India and the U.S.

Professional Appointments: I have worked as a journalist for United News of India, Hindustan Times, Times of India and Outlook magazine.

Honors:

- Outstanding Research Contribution Award at University of Tennessee. (2017)
- CCI-Best Research Award (student-faculty collaboration) at the University of Tennessee. (2016)
- Travel grant from CCI to present research paper at AEJMC international conference. (2016)
- Reeder-Siler Fellowship at the University of Tennessee. (2016)
- Karl and Madira Bickel Scholarship at the University of Tennessee. (2015)
- ESPN Sports Media Fellowship at the University of Tennessee. (2014)
- 'Certificate of Appreciation' from the U.S. State Department for Diplomacy Lab project. (2015)
- FASPE Ethics Fellowship for the study of journalistic ethical lapses during the Second World War, sponsored by the Jewish Museum of Heritage in New York, USA. (2013)
- Marilyn Miller Kaytor Fellowship at the University of Illinois in Urbana-Champaign. (2012)
- Achievement Award by India's largest English-language daily Hindustan Times. (2009)

Publications from the Last 3 Years:

Anjalin, U., Mazumdar, A. & White, E. (2017). Asian Students' Experience of Culture Shock and Coping Strategies. *Journal of Education and Social Development*, *1*(1), 7-13.

Mazumdar, A. (2017). Dial H for hatred: Did *Independent* conclude too soon it's a hate crime? *Journal of Global Communication, 10*(1),1-9.

Mazumdar, A. (2016). Paid news in India disrupts press freedom and ethical conduct. *International Communication Research Journal, 51*(2), 43-67.

Mazumdar, A. (2016). Pakistan media: Unnamed sources reveal political crises and law and order problems. *Central European Journal of Communication, 9*(2), 213-228.

Mazumdar, A. & Harmon, M. (2016). The Press Complaints Commission is Dead; Long Live the IPSO? *Journal of Global Communication, 9*(2), 74-81.

Mazumdar, A. (2016). A comparative study of social media guidelines of media organizations. *Journal of Media Studies, 31*(2), 100-126.

Mazumdar, A. (2015). Common themes in the news from anonymous sources in Indian political reporting. *Journal of Global Communication, 8*(2), 105-113.

In: Advances in Sociology Research   ISBN: 978-1-53616-781-8
Editor: Jared A. Jaworski   © 2020 Nova Science Publishers, Inc.

Chapter 7

WHO IS (NOT) INDIVIDUAL: INDIVIDUALISM, INDIVIDUALITY, AND NEGATION

Predrag Krstić
Institute for Philosophy and Social Theory,
University of Belgrade, Serbia

ABSTRACT

The article discusses dilemmas of understing the individual, which are presented through a scene from *Monty Python's Life of Brian*. The speech which Brian delievers to his assembled followers and the reactions to it amusingly display typical conceptual problems arising in both the Englightment's 'ideology of individualism' – which claims that the individual is oppossed to the collective and above it – and its arguable follow-up, the Romantic favoring of 'individuality'. Special attention is given to the dynamic journey of both imposing and expanding the individuality of a single personality, to the point of having it 'swallowed up' in supra-personal entities. The conclusion suggests that contemporary understandings of the 'individual' have shifted from 'final indivisibility' to negation of every subsummation, including the one that affirms it, at the price of a paradox that bears witness to its fragile theoretical construction.

INTRODUCTION

According to the charming historical reinterpretation of the spirit of the New Testament times, offered in 1979 by the Monty Python's "Flying Circus" in the satirical film *Life of Brian*, Brian Cohen Maximus was born on the same day as Jesus Christ in the manger next door. In a "Parallel Biography," which allows one to parody the story of Jesus from a safe distance – especially its historical influence (Mayordomo 2011: 55) – we are witnesses to his ensuing fate: he is constantly and unshakenly being mistaken for the messiah. But Brian has grown up into a reasonably prudent guy, or rather, to a one who does not wish to be the messiah nor to have any followers whatsoever: "an average guy who just wants to live a quiet life" (Benko 2012: 6).

Giordano Vintaloro (2008) offered possibly the boldset and most cynical interpretation of Brian's negation of his own messiasness, recognizing in him a model for modern leadership. Along the same line with Vintaloro – and less interested in the political pragmatism of the leader than in the structure of those being led – Mayordomo believes that what is viewed most clearly in the absurd status of the involuntary saviour is that a principally impossible doctrine of Brian, "Brianology," would have to depend on the "unconditional will of the religiously fanatic audience to wrongly understand" (Mayordomo 2011: 64-65; cf. Huss 2006: 148). However, Steven Benko is not so convinced that there can not be found at least implicitly, if not a Brianology, than a clearly evidenced outlook advocated by Brian, and thus susceptible to counterfeiting: defying everything and everyone, in order to achieve the desired ideal – to become an individual and gain freedom to determine one's own meaning of life (Benko 2012: 13-14).

THE INDESCREET CHARM OF FOLLOWSHIP

Brian goes through various misfortunate adventures, but one is crucial for his 'carrier' of the controverter of the 'choseness' and the mentality that it produces. Just as he believed that he had slipped away from his admiriers who irrevocably refered to him as the messiah the previous day, he is greeted in the morning outside his house by a crowd filling the square. He openes the window and is dumbfound at what he sees. Since his previous attempts to talk them out of followship was to no avail, Brian decides to give the speech they ask from him, and take advantage of the trust and impact he enjoys to convert them forever. First he wishes them: "Good morning." The crowd cheers: "*A blessing! A blessing!*," creating at the very start a situation of asymmetric communication between the believers and the high priest. Brian rejects this division of roles immidietly. "No. No, please! Please! Please listen." The crowd is completely silent, yearningly awaiting, as Brian makes the introduction: "I've got one or two things to say." The unified choir wholeheartedly chants a two-fold reply: "Tell us. Tell us both of them." Then Brian gets straight to the point: "Look. You've got it all wrong" – and continues his explanation expressively in the same breath: "You don't need to follow me. You don't need to follow anybody!" As required by rhetorical customs, it is time for the silenced crowd to hear what they have to do: "You've got to think for yourselves." The point is finally made with what the crowd ought to become, or what it already is, but does not realize it yet: "You're all individuals!" The crowd then readily, unanimously and in a thundering voice, accepts this claim, whose pronounciation makes it seem as a performative contradiction: "Yes, we're all individuals!". Whether to sharpen the message and make the crowd accept the principles that deny it, or out of desperation, Brian adds something which is somewhere between a demand and autogenic training: "You're all different!". Those adressed find that this is a truely convinient reason to rhythmically incantate: "Yes, we are all different!". But then, just beneath the window where Brian is holding his speech, Dennis occurs, a quiet voice under the hood, who with a slight lift of his hand turns the situation upside down once again and denies the already impossible: "I'm not [different]." The crowd silences him (Chapman et al. 1997: 46).

The dialogue between Brian and his followers, apart from becoming an abbrevation for certain situations under the colloquial code "You/We're all individuals," recieved its theoretical interpretations, or served as a useful illustration of various reflections. Some emphasized the first turn, the collective vow that we are all individuals. Thus, Luther Martin finds that Brian's imploring persuading of his diligent pupils that they do not have to depend on him or anybody else, with what the crowd unanimously agrees, is ironically raising the "the perennial question of the relationship between self and society: Is the self to be understood, ideally, as an autonomous subject, or is the identity of the self in reality a social construct contingent upon its membership in some corporate body?" (Martin 1994: 118). The author is unequivocally in favour of the second answer and demonstrates convincingly that the Pythonic "parodic portrayal of an individualistic assertion rejected by the affirming discourse of a collective subject" is not only principally possible, but also that it accuratelly summarized the core feature of Helenistic culture (Martin 1994: 118). He refutes the popular thesis that "Man as a political animal, a fraction of the *polis*" had ended with Aristotle, and that with Alexander the Macedonian's conquests and political internationalism emerged "Man as an individual" and – individualism (Tarn 193). The cultural transformation which had undoubtedly marked the Helenistic era could have "occasioned a heightened awareness of the empirical individual," he agrees, but he also insists that any claim that such existension could be 'ideologicaly' valued, in the sense of advocting some sort of 'individualism,' is making the classic error of attributing contemporary values and theorethical boundaries to a time and people they do not belong to: Helenism does not value such existence in any way, nor does it find it significant (Martin 1994: 121).

Contrary to the promises of the modern ideology of individualism, the only "promise of individualism characteristic of Hellenistic culture was that of the social exclusion and lonely isolation," an "asocial, diminished state of being," the 'wandering' that reveals its ill-fate, from Sofocles *Edipoe* to Apulio's novel *The Golden Ass* (Martin 1994: 127). Surely, historians can continue disputing when the "'ideal' of the individual self" was constructed for the first time out of empirical reality and 'collectively valued,' in contrast to the ideal of a 'corporate subject,' and social theorist to linger in their attemts to grasp "to what extent an ideology of individualism ever actually produces an autonomous individual subject," and isn't it too, like every other ideology, just another "social strategy of subjection," but what is certian, Martin believes, is that for the Greeks and Romans every concept of modern Western individualism was "irrelevant:" "Their ideas and icons, discourse and practices, acts and gestures all confirm the anti-individualistic and collective character of a shared cultural ideal" (Martin 1994: 133-134).

Still, in a social psychological research which comprises the claim *We're all individuals* in its title, it is demonstrated that it's not unusual even for contemporary individualistic cultures to have an anti-individualistic and collective nature, and that individualism can be normatively prescribed quite appropriately and accepted by acclamation, as in *The Life of Brian*. Some sort of the working hypothesis – that "the degree of conformity to group norms of collectivism or individualism varies as a function of group members' commitment to the group" (Jetten, Postmes & Mcauliffe 2002: 190) – was confirmed, and with it the existence of 'Brian's paradox:' it is possible to be a wholehearted member of a group with individualistic norms. For example, in a culture traditionally viewed as the most individualistic in the world (cf. Hofstede 1980), those Americans who greatly identify with their affiliation put great emphasis on their individuality, contrary to their compatriots who don't have this level of national identification. So not only is it imaginable, but there is also a contradiction at work in the claim that "the outcome of strong identification with a group is the pursuit of an individualist goal" (Jetten, Postmes & Mcauliffe 2002: 192).

Thus, according to the most striking result of this research, it is possible to simultaniously be both very commited to a group and to define oneself as an 'individual' who acts 'individualistically.' What researchers are suggesting is that people who identify themselves to a large degree with a nation or some other group whose dominant culture is individualistic tend to adopt the social identity of an 'individual.' Individualistic cultures are therefore not individualistic "in the sense of being impervious to social influences of social groups and of their culture, but as demonstrating collectivism through strong individualism" (Jetten,

Postmes & Mcauliffe 2002: 204). Accomodating to a group that cherishes the norm of individualism largely explains "the paradox that social influence can be powerful in a society where everyone claims to be independent and autonomous" (Jetten, Postmes & Mcauliffe 2002: 189). In this sense, it is concluded that it would be instructive to take into account "the collective dimension of individualism," i.e., the cultural production of the 'individual self,' usually percieved as a personal accomplishement: "When we hear people argue that 'we are all individuals', this may disguise (and paradoxically convey at the same time) the underlying social influence that permits individualism to endure" (Jetten, Postmes & Mcauliffe 2002: 205).

Other commentators focus on the other turn, or the second step of the Brian's 'sermon' conondrum – to that seemingly nonsense moment when an individual member of the group defies the already paradoxical belonging to the collective of indivuduals. Thus Benko finds that the joke is that Brian, forced to speak, asks from a crowd of people gathered outside his window to become individuals, while the crowd continues to agree unanimously – except its one member who declares that he is not an individual and for whome it seems at first to actualy be the only one for that very reason. At second glance, however, he gains company. "Ironically," Benko concludes, "the only true individuals were Brian, the lone dissenter in the crowd who denied his individuality and, eventually, anyone who sees through the irony to the truth conveyed in that joke" (Benko 2012: 9-10).

Let's leave aside those observers for whom it is already difficult to establish if they are getting the 'truth' of the joke with sufficient irony. Brian too, having unwillingly accepted the role of the speaker, takes an anti-individualistic tone or, at least, one directed to the collective, contradicting the content of his speech and putting him in a situational paradox, even before the choir of believers confronts him with it. Schilbrack (2006: 17) allows for a moment the possibility that Brian's entire tirade is only a 'tuning up' for the joke, consisting in the lonely answer from the crowd "I'm not!" to his reasurance that "You're all different!," for that 'nice little paradox,' given that Dennis "both rejects

Brian's teaching and accepts it at the same time, whereas all the rest who follow the crowd in accepting Brian's teaching actually fail to accept it." But he quickly denies that this might be the motivation on part of the author and suggest that the issue is something more far-reaching than an ordinary joke, that Brian is sincere while making a speech from the window, that they are his real thoughts, a certain Brian's 'philosophy' that has at least one principle: one ought to be an individual, to think for oneself, and not be a follower. The affirmation that this, indeed, is the "message that the Pythons wanted to send" is firstly acknowledged in "the passion in Brian's voice" and his "pained look" during the speech, and afterwards in Michael Palin's comment that *The Life of Brian* reflects "the basis of what Python comedy was all about, which is really resisting people telling you how to behave and how not to behave:" "It was the freedom of the individual, a very Sixties thing, the independence which was part of the way Python had been formed" (Chapman et al. 2003: 306). But Schilbrack rightfully reminds us that Brian's sermon reflects not only the 1960s, but represents the "principle basic to most modern philosophy, and especially the eighteenth-century movement called the Enlightenment, namely, the principle that individuals should think for themselves" (Schilbrack 2006: 17), the motto *philosophes* that Kant summed up in the credo: "*Sapere aude!* Have courage to use your own reason!" (Kant 1968: 35).

YOU/WE'RE ALL INDIVIDUALS

The 'discovery' of the independently thinking individual can be (ante)dated differently: it can be ascribed to Homer, if we bear in mind his heroes Achilles or Odysseus (Pelling 1990: v; Horkheimer & Adorno 1997: 53-82), to lyric poets and Greek mystery cults from the 6th century B.D. (Snell 1982; Burkert 1987: 11), Plato's depiction of Socrates (Garland 1992: 134), Roman poets of the Hellenistic age and Augustine, the 11th or the 12th century (Morris 1972), Renaissance Italy (Burckhardt 1869), the 16th and the 17th century (Trilling 1972), or, finally, to the 18th century

(Woolf 1931). On the other hand, it has been reasonably emphasized that an 'empirical' individual – as a specific example of humanity which is the "subject of speech, thought, and will," and which can be found in all societies – is one thing, and that 'ideological' individualism, which values "the independent, autonomous, and thus essentially nonsocial moral being, who carries...[the] permanent values" (Dumont 1986: 25), is another. Confusing "a social acknowledgement of individual" with "the social valuing of individuals above the collective of which they are member," while making a historical reconstruction is attributing individualism too boldly, as a force that gathers and affirms truely existing individuals, even there where it didn't exist.

'Individual' as an object of historical observation is, in other words, not the same as a 'person' as the construct of cultural and historical context (Mauss 1985), i.e., it is not the same as the "system of ideas and values" which affirms it in the "given social milieu" and which could be labelled "ideology" (Dumont 1986: 9). 'Ideology of individualism' thus refers to those social constructs that put the individual, now advanced to a 'personality,' above the collective.[9] Besides, 'individualism' is also a late lexical discovery. *Individualisme* is a 19th century French term, derived from the adjective *individuel*, which has, addmitedly, been in use since at least 1490 (Guilbert, Lagane & Niobey 1975: 2592; Lecourt 2004: 11-12), and afterwards, in lack of another equivalent, *individualism* appears in the English language in 1840, with the 1835 translation of Tocqueville's *Democracy in America* (cf. Tocqueville 1900: 104; Lukes 1973: 3-16; Martin 1994: 119).[10]

What seems certain than is that, if not the first appearance of the 'individual,' then the first doctrinal affirmation of the individual who is no longer integrated into the collective – or even one which opposes and desintegrates it – marked the 18th century turn to Modernism, which meant

---

[9] For this discussion, based on the both theoretical and historical distinction between the empirical individual and its individualistic construction, see Lukes 1973; Kippenberg, Kuiper & Sanders.

[10] 'Individualism' is not mentioned even in its most articulate social apology – in the essay *On Freedom*, published in 1859, John Stuart Mill constantly uses the term *individuality*, celebrating it and advocating it in a noticeable 'individualistic' fashion (Mill 2001: 52-59, 66).

decisive parting from inherited ways of thinking and acting (cf. Luhmann 1986; Ehrenberg 1995; Ireland 2004). Until then, in the perspective of pre-Modern societies, the 'individual' was (dis)qualified in advance, and 'individualistic' behaviour was viewed as deviant and/or idiotic. Not only was there no contemporary emphasis on personal individuality, but it was also probably unimaginable for Middle Age Europe's self-understaning: society functioned on the basis of status and other attributes defined by birth, which invariably determined man's position in the community. People weren't considered unique individuals with an identity of their own, but part of the 'Great Chain of Being.' Everything that exists has its place in the order of things: God is at the top, beneath him are rulers and less important human beings, and at the bottom there are animals, plants, and inanimate objects. In that sense, the individual truely "did not exist in traditional cultures" (Giddens 1991: 75).

The authentic 'phenomenon' of Modernism is the positive assessment of a indiviual that is both opposed to previous experience and constituted by it (cf. Beck 2002: 27). Only with the appearance of contemporary societies and, particularaly, with differentiations based on the division of labour did the isolated individual come to the center of attention, Baumeister (1986: 29) concludes as well. Macintyre would suggest that man had been understood in functional terms in the classical tradition, and that with the undermining and rejection of the tradition a certain social defunctionalizatiton of man came about: instead of recognizing humanity as fulfilling a set of roles that have their point and purpose – "member of a family, citizen, soldier, philosopher, servant of God" – appears "an individual prior to and apart from all roles" (Macintyre 2007: 59). Therefore, the context and the hierarchical structure of the world order are lost for the (in)dubious benefit of liberating oneself from teistic obscurantism and gaining autonomy.

The Cartesian individual becomes a unique, unified rational personality, capable of thinking with its own head and understanding the world independently. He/she is different and isolated from others – who are also self-governing – and is not bounded by his/her position in society or by traditional beliefs. "The Enlightenment subject was based on a conception of the human person as a fully centred, unified individual, endowed with the capacities of reason, consciousness and action" (Hall 1992: 275). After possibly the first 'individual,' Milton's Satan, whose principle *Non serviam* stands up against every established hierarchy, the generations of Rousseau and Smith now found their Bible in Daniel Defoe's *Robinson Crusoe*. Basically, this novel embodies the Enlightenment individualism that favours personal experience and believes it can overcome every situaton by the means of its own strenght (Fohrmann 1981; Macintyre 1998: 97; Macintyre 2007: 261). The modern man thus becomes *homo faber*, and social life an arena in which conflicted individual wills battle.[11]

In short, individuals are understood by emerging Modernism as independant, rational beings who prescribe their own outlooks to themselves. The individual agent, liberated from every hierarchy and teleology, can now, for real or for imaginary, imagine himself as sovereign in his affairs. However things stand with his fabrication, the consequences of his discoursive establishment had a social 'dialectic' of their own. The utopia of 'extreme individualism' of the French philosophers of the Englightment has recently transformed into – to use Talmon's words – a "collective pattern of coercion before the eighteenth century was out" and now, in a 'tragic paradox,' "instead of bringing about, as it promised, a system of final and permanent stability, it gave rise to utter restlessness, and in place of a reconciliation between human freedom and social

---

[11] A (arche)formulation of this status of the individual was offered by John Locke in 1689: "every man has a 'property' in his own 'person.' This nobody has any right but to himself" (Locke 1823: 116). For a vision of personal and social organization where the individual is defined by 'capacity' to stand beyond himself, to separate 'self' from the rest of 'body' and to possess himself as a person, a new phrase was established – 'possessive individualism' – suggesting that the epithet determines the noun better and discloses it (Macpherson 1962: 1-2, 12). But the conceptual frame is not by any means new, nor is it left unspoken of: "In the early modern period the property/selfhood interconnection must have appeared almost tautological; one word for *property* was *propriety* deriving from the Latin *proprius*, that is, own or peculiar to oneself. What is proper to oneself is that which – existentially and etymologically! – one owns" (Gunn 1995: 48; cf. Davies 1998; Pateman 1988). Indeed, already Comte Antoine Destutt de Tracy, an aristocrat and a philosopher of the early French Enlightenment, demonstrates that *proprieté*, *individualité* and *personalité* are the same: "nature has endowed man with an inevitable and inalienable property, property in the form of his own individuality" (Tracy 1970: 100).

cohesion, it brought totalitarian coercion" (Talmon 1952: 252; Talmon 1959: 151).

The scene when Brian makes the speech from his home window could be useful when elaborating this complex adventure of the individual. For beyond its local instructiveness of this kind or the other, beyond understanding it as a poignant subversion, as a contemporary downhearted provocation with the ambition of vague emancipation, as a pun that revitalizes the grotesque genre, as an affirmation of humor in praise of the comforting or proud-spirited community of viewers who have the privilege to hold an ironic stance,[12] his speech bears testimony – in a manner more successful and certainly more picturesque and conspicuous – to the characteristic vertiginous clashing of epochal concepts, pregnant with an accumulated history of problems, with their own limitation, to their turmoil and depletion, until they distort to their opposition and/or to nonsense. One answer to such a cardinal disorientation is laughter, the other is crying, and both acknowledge the bankruptcy of discursive operators and the helplesness in the world (Plessner 1950). But maybe it is possible to simultaniosuly, or at least after this reaction – which is guaranteed laughter in the case of the Python's – analyse what actually happened and where the 'wrong turn' was made. For, there is some unpathethic or antipathetic, surely joyeus, but also skillful confrontation of conceptions with their own truth in the caricatures displayed by the Python's, there is an exposing of the inner contradictions of the concepts, which through defamiliarization and situational displacement, by being amusingly turned upside down and processed in a parodic fashion, become more emphasized and, for that reason, both questionable and instructive.[13] An amusing conondrum, inspired by the potentially theorethically fruitfull approach to its punctuating and dissolution, will innevitably become less effective, but at

---

[12] On the revival of the grotesque and carnival spirit in Monthy Python, see Bishop 1990: esp. 53-55; on the potential for emancipation of the 'buffoon comedy' of the Pythons and the moderately liberated 'community of the ironists' inspired by their achievement: Erickson 2006: 118; Benko 2012: 16-17.

[13] What is probably closest to this sort of understanding is the observation that in the satirical saga of the *Life* there are some 'unbearable oppositions' – which can be resolved only by the means of laughter (Auxier 2006: 72; Mayordomo 2011: 65).

the same time the idea is not to pacify its sharp; in a sense, quite the opposite – to make it deadlier by emphasizing its paradoxalistic right.

YOU'RE ALL DIFFERENT

The trajectory of the historical turn from 'individualism' to 'collectivism' is rather specific: the latter is reached not throught direct, irreconcilable and unfruitful opposing the former as a 'reciprocal concept' (Adorno 1997: 279; Macintyre 2007: 34-35) – as in the case of some evergreen modern political alternative – but just the opposite, or so to speak, by means of forcing and tempting individualism, until it is comes to stand as its own opposition. At the end of the 18th century, a desired norm was already formulated as a claim that every individual is different and original, and that his or her 'originality' determines how he or she ought to live (Taylor 2006: 376). This sharpening of the logic of 'individuation' and simultaniously hypostatizing the individual until it fades away in this or that particular generality is usually detected as precisely the leap that marks the transition' from Enlightment to Romanticism.

This turn could be called the turn from 'individualism' to – 'individuality. The conception of individualism would belong to the Enlightenment period, as in fact a kind of authentic ideology of the individual, while individuality (*Individualität*) would be a creation of the Romantic-era. The nativity of both terms could be therefore put in the 18th century, but there is no consent on whether they appear as entirely new discursive and social formations and specifically modern epochal transformations, or as a crown of particular historical movements which could only at the expence of an explanation ahistorically deny their own tradition. Either way, the latter paronym was characteristic only of the German language. Now once again, in a crucial turn, 'individuality' opposes 'individualism' that unifies individuals in terms of the implied universal aspiration.

According to the Romantic understanding or feeling, the Englighteners reduced mankind to a set of principally similar beings that possess universal rights and that are motivated by similar needs. This conception was abstracted from the modern, market-oriented society, where every individual pursues its own, personal interest, although uniform in terms of it's nature. One could say that an affirmation of 'individuality' emerged from this individualism of the Enlightement, therby changing the original idea and turning it against its own source. After the "thorough liberation of the individual from the rusty chains of guild, birthright and church," Georg Simmel writes, the now 'independent' individual desired also to "distinguish himself from other individuals: The important point no longer was the fact that he was a free individual as such, but that he was this specific, irreplaceable given individual" (Simmel 1950: 78). Simmel suggest that the 'new individualism' should be called 'qualitative' or the individualism of 'uniqueness' (*Einzigkeit*), in contrast to 'quantitative,' i.e., the individualism of 'singleness' (*Einzelheit*) (Simmel 1950: 78, 80–81).

But the key moment of the 'turn' happened with an unexpected, not denial, but transposition of the seemingly simple and persistent affirmation of the individual – his unique and irreducable individuality. If everyone ought to pursue an original path, and if, in return, every person should be assessed differently and according to appropriate individualized standards, "why should it not also be true for each human being in particular?," asks Taylor (2006: 376). Thus already in the proto-Romantism of Herder, the 'notion of originality as a vocation' had spreaded in an examplary manner from the individual to understanding national cultures: "Different *Völker* have their own way of being human, and shouldn't betray it by aping others" (Taylor 2006: 376). Romanticism both generalized singularities and universalized their particularity and – inaugurated a certain radical 'nominalism' of the images of life and the creations of culture. During this turn, the individuality of the person spreads into an seemingly, at least until then, *contradictio in adjecto* – into a 'supra-personal individuality' – presuming now the individuality of every culture as well.[14]

This concept of the individuality of collective entities was succeded by possibly the most peculiar Romantic idea: that personal individuality

---

[14] Such 'cultural pluralism' of the 18th century Romantic historicism develops into a fascination with the 'local coloring': "the region is a concretization of a local, individual, unique coloring of life" – Maria Janion argues – „Not of life 'in general', although Romanticism was also very interested in that issue, but life as it is 'there'." (Janjion 1976: 138, 234).

developes and ultimatilly affirms itself precisely by identifying the individual with the unique properties of the culture it belongs to. The sort of middle term in this quantificator play was rather a feeling of disunity than a conscious insight that if an individual were to be understood independently of the collective or opposed to it, then the complete harmony of the individual and the whole would be lacking, the very harmony to which the Romantics – presuming its implied desirability – wholeheartedly strived to. Distancing itself from the 18th century individualism of the Englighteners – who supposedly imagined a society of atomizied individuals, isolated from other equal individuals and competing with them – the Romantics concept of individuality now wishes, somehow together with radical dissimilation, the individuation of individuals, non-contradictory to presuppose an extension of such peculiarities from individuals to groups, and a harmonic drowning into a high(est) totality. Friedrich Meinecke finds that in the "deepening of the individualism of uniqueness" in Germany, "new and powerful ideas" emerged in many ways and in various forms, and with it "a novel and livlier image of the state, as well as a new image of the world: It seemed that the whole world was now filled with individuality, and that every individuality, personal or supra-personal, was lead by one's own life principles... Individuality everywhere, the identity of mind and nature, and through that identity an invisible but strong link that unites otherwise disconnected diversity and richness of a singular phenomenon" (Meinecke 1957: 425). Individuality thus advanced to mark a specific collective identity – and primarily a German one.

The essential features and contradictions of the concept of 'individuality' can though be detected in the writtings of the English and French Romanticists. All the early Romanticists, without exception, have focused their tribulation on a unique individual and often, more specifically, on their own histories. Not giving up on the expansion of the infinite personal self, by means of reformulating and simultaniously redislocating it, they have attempted nontheless to tame that particular 'individuality' – which now enters into a relationship and unites with some kind of an *all-inclusive* totality, other and bigger than self (Izenberg 1992:

50-51). However, only the German Romantics expanded and tranformed the notion of the souvereign personal individual – the notion of individual by which Schlegel meant "the continuous becoming in an unfinished world," finding Leibneitz-wise that "every individuum is a new word for the universe" (Schlegel 1964: 42, 101; cf. Nassar 2013: 98) – into the notion of, one could also say, a personified supra-individual entity, i.e., in the image of a national or state 'personality.' The issue regarding this transition from a singular to a collective individuality is "an abyss to be bridged rather than a bridge to be crossed," Izenberg warnes: "paradox, or more accurately, contradiction," that the Romantics' conception of individuality firstly emphasized "differences among unique individuals" for which it seemed to "rule out any kind of nonconflictual organic synthesis between self and other or self and collective identity," that they valued the individual even beyond the regional borders of economic or moral acts as "striving for infinite freedom," that they never stopped with personal questioning, experimenting and self-expansion of the open end, and that in time the meaning of individuality shifted to "closure," implying the "total integration of self and community or state" – "is the heart of European Romanticism, not just in Germany and not just in politics" (Izenberg 1992: 5–6).

CONCLUSION: I'M NOT

Contradiction and paradox are nevertheless logical categories. The entire set of emergence, development and mutation of the 'individual' could probably be reduced to variations in emphasis in those elementary logic concentric circles that mark the relation of the singular, particular and general: the smallest represents the singular (individual), the medium the particular, the biggest the general (universal). It seems that trouble occurs with the historical (self)understanding of the particular – not the most general, nor the most singular. The trouble is that the particular, as a sort of mediator, has the 'natural' tendency to negate and abolish on its own account that which it mediates – both universality and individuality – so it produces and passes itself for both solely wholly and solely indivisible. Contemporarly politicly speaking – Finkielkraut is right – the Romanticist argumentation is focused against two "black sheep: individualism and cosmopolitism: the national genius abolishes simultaniously the individual (dissolved in the group from which he originates) and humanity (fragmented into stiff essences, dispersed into a multitude of ethnic personalities which are closed into themselves). And if the denial of the individual gives birth to infinite governement, from the disintegration of the human species, a total war is born" (Finkelkrot 1993: 46).

However, in the historico-political sense, this particularity which also emphasized excellence was called *Sonderweg*, and is associated to the *Die deutsche Bewegung* of pre-Romantism and Romantism from 1770 to 1830, for which, according to Meinecke's reconstruction, the triumph of historicims was crucial.[15] The motto of Meinecke's entire capital piece on the emergence of historism from 1936 was taken from Goethe's letter to Lavater from September 20, 1780, in which the latter is thrilled with the expression *individuum est ineffabile* and claims that the "world is deduced" from it (Goethe 1961: 533; Meinecke 1965: 7; cf. Heller 1986: 108; Jannidis 1996; Kemper 2004). Since 'individual' characteristics of newly established collective entities have to be clearly distinguished from characteristics of other formations, the neighbourhood benchmark constantly colored the German attempts to define the specific form of 'individualism,' which is not only different, but also superior compared to the shallow, mechanic and materialistic individualism of Britain and France. Their utilitarianism and liberalism is confronted by the German regard for the unrepeatable uniqueness and spirituality of a different kind of genius, regard for the *Bildung* in all its cultural and moral meanings, and with all its social and political concequences. Authentic German culture, opposed to 'Western civilazation,' had to lay on other, ultimately not in the slightest 'individualistic' foundations.

That's how through advocating 'individuality' to a level of paroxysm, and through simultaneous justification of the particularization of precisely

---

[15] For the reconstruction and deconstruction of the *Sonderweg* idea and the "The German movement", see Meinecke 1965; Nohl 1970; Fulda 2005; Oergel 2006.

the otherwise universally individualistic nature of cultural entities, the 'individual' came full circle and restored power to its opposition. Maistre is quite frank about this. Everything that the individualism of Englightement attributed to the autocratic individual must be true of nations: they are "born and die like individuals" (Maistre 2012: 99). They are a political collective that is truly final, original and indivisible, the Greek α-τόμων which, by following an unsual trajectory through the Latin translation *in-dividuum*, was attributed together with the ideology of individualism to the sovereignty of the individual personality, and – almost simultaniously – through both the conservative reaction and the Romantic escalation, dissmised from it on behalf of what it was believed it had sprung out from.

The (late) Romanticism came to a classic conservative understanding which implies absolute primacy of society over the individual and, so to say, went hand in hand with it (cf., for example, Maistre 1996: 87–88; Bonald 1859: 163, 1074-1075). And hence Adam Müller understands the Englightement idea of becoming independent by conquering individual autonomy as a fataly dangerous error. The individual cannot free itself from social ties and take a stance outside of society, in order to establish the order of things again. He cannot pull himself out of the chains of history, put himself "at the beginning or the end of all time," but is truly immersed in time. Finally, the individual cannot use politics for achieving its personal goals, and treat the state as sort of a 'insurance company.' People are produced by history and politics, not the other way round (Müller 2006: 38–39).

And just there is where the seemingly inserted replica in *The Life of Brian*, which looks like it serves to once again rotate the basic joke – the "I am not" (different), shyly spoken out by a low-spirited fellow from the crowd before being shut up – gains its right. The moment of the claim confuting its own content bears witness not so much, or not only, to a performative contradiction, but to the genuine paradox of being signified as an individual – in plural; maybe even to the ancient lesson that reminds us of the insufficiency of every discursive processing and treatment of the singular. And, having acknowledged the manufactureness of the unique individual – whether human or 'cultural,' whether in or opposed to whatever generality it might find itself, being it factual or conceptual – what other remains for it to do but to go beyond origin and pursue its own affirmation by denying this composure and compacteness, in the self-identification which is inevitabily, like every other determination, always distinguishing, always the denial of isomorphism and belonging, in the non-exeptance or resistance to every summarized subordination and institutionalization, or even designation, in the constant process of differentiating, which is disciplinary and not accidentaly called "the principle of individuation" (Leibniz 1982: 229-231)? And this is true, or is particulary true, of speaking or theoretizing in its name.

REFERENCES

Adorno, Theodor W. (1997). *Negative Dialektik/Jargon der Eigentlichkeit* [*Negative Dialectics/The Jargon of Authenticity*]. Adorno: Gesammelte Schriften, vol. 6. Frankfurt am Main: Suhrkamp.

Auxier, Randall E. (2006). "A Very Naughty Boy. Getting Right with Brian." In *Monty Python and Philosophy: Nudge Nudge, Think Think!* Eds. Gary L. Hardcastle & George A. Reisch. Chicago: Open Court, pp. 65-81.

Baumeister, Roy F. (1986). *Identity: Cultural Change and the Struggle for Self*. Oxford: Oxford University Press.

Benko, Steven A. (2012). "Ironic Faith in Monty Python's Life of Brian." *Journal of Religion & Film* 16: article 6: 0-20. http://digitalcom mons.unomaha.edu/cgi/viewcontent.cgi?article=1010&context=jrf (Accessed 7 Apr. 2016).

Beck, Ulrich (2002). "A Life of One's Own in a Runaway World: Individualization, Globalization and Politics." In *Individualisation: Institucionalized Individualism and its Social and Political Consequences*. Eds. Ulrich Beck & Elisabeth Beck-Gernsheim. London: SAGE, pp. 22-29.

Bishop, Ellen (1990). "Bakhtin, Carnival and Comedy: The New Grotesque in Monty Python and the Holy Grail." *Film Criticism* 15 (1): 49-64.

Bonald, Louis Gabriel Ambroise (1859). *Oeuvres Completes [Complete Works]*, vol 1. Ed. Abbe Jacques-Paul Migne. Paris: Migne, https://catalog.hathitrust.org/
Record/011601763 (Accessed 31 June, 2017).

Burkert, Walter (1987). *Ancient Mystery Cults*. Cambridge: Harvard University Press.

Burckhardt, Jacob (1869). *Die Cultur der Renaissance in Italien [The Civilization of the Renaissance in Italy]*. Leipzig: E. A. Seemann, https://babel.hathitrust.org/cgi/pt?id=hvd.
hwjs9v;view=1up;seq=7 (Accessed 12 Jan. 2015).

Chapman, Graham, John Cleese, Terry Gilliam, Eric Idle, Terry Jones, Michael Palin (1979). *The Life of Brian – Monty Python Scrapbook*. London: Eyre Methuen.

Chapman, Graham, John Cleese, Terry Gilliam, Eric Idle, Terry Jones, Michael Palin, with Bob McCabe (2003). *The Pythons Autobiography by The Pythons*. London: Orion.

Davies, Margaret (1998). "The Proper: Dicourses of Purity." *Law and Critique* 9 (2): 147–173..

Dumont, Louis (1986). *Essays on Individualism*. Chicago: University of Chicago Press.

Ehrenberg, Alain (1995). *L'Individu incertain [The Uncertain Individual]*. Paris: Calmann-Levy.

Erickson, Stephen (2006). "Is There Life After Monty Python's *Meaning of Life?*" In *Monty Python and Philosophy: Nudge Nudge, Think Think!* Eds. Gary L. Hardcastle & George A. Reisch. Chicago: Open Court, pp. 111-122.

Finkelkrot, Alen (1993). *Poraz mišljenja [The Defeat of the Mind]*. Beograd: XX vek.

Fohrmann, Jürgen (1981). *Abenteuer und Bürgertum: zur Geschichte der deutschen Robinsonaden im 18. Jahrhundert [Adventure and*

Bourgeoisie: The History of the German Robinsonades in the 18th Century]. Stuttgart: Metzler.

Fulda, Daniel (2005). "Literary Criticism and Historical Science: The Textuality of History in the Age of Goethe – and Beyond." In *The Discovery of Historicity in German Idealism and Historism*. Ed. Peter Koslowski. Berlin: Springer, pp. 112–133.

Garland, Robert (1992). *Introducing New Gods: The Politics of Athenian Religion*. Ithaca: Cornell University Press.

Giddens, Anathony (1991). *Modernity and Self-Identity. Self and Society in the Late Modern Age*. Cambridge: Polity Press.

Goethe, Johann Wolfgang von (1961). *Gedenkausgabe der Werke* [*Commemorative Edition of the Works*]. Briefe und Gespräche [Letters and conversations], vol. 18. Ed. Ernst Beutler. Zürich: Artemis.

Guilbert, Louis, René Lagane & Georges Niobey (Eds.) (1975). *Grand Larousse de la langue française* [*Grand Larousse Encyclopedia of the French Language*], vol. 4. Paris: Librairie Larousse, http://gallica. bnf.fr/ark:/12148/bpt6k1200535k/f41.item.r=individual (Accessed 1 Sep. 2014).

Gunn, Richard (1995). "What Do We Owe to the Scots: Reflections on Caffentzis, the Property Form and Civilisation." *Common Sense* 17: 39-68.

Hall, Stuart (1992). "The Question of Cultural Identity." In *Modernity and its Futures*. Eds. Stuart Hall, David Held & Anthony G. McGrew. Cambridge: Polity Press, pp. 274-316.

Heller, Thomas S. (1986). *Reconstructiong Individualism: Autonomy, Individuality, and the Self in Western Thought*. Stanford: Stanford University Press.

Hofstede G. (1980). *Culture's Consequences: Comparing Values, Behaviors, Institutions and Organizations*. Beverly Hills: SAGE.

Horkheimer, Max & Theodor W. Adorno (1997). *Dialektik der Aufklärung* [*Dialectic of Enlightenment*]. Adorno: Gesammelte Schriften, vol. 3. Frankfurt am Main: Suhrkamp.

Huss, John (2006). "Monty Python and David Hume on Religion." In *Monty Python and Philosophy: Nudge Nudge, Think Think!* Eds. Gary L. Hardcastle & George A. Reisch. Chicato: Open Court, pp. 141-152.

Ireland, Craig (2004). *Subaltern Appeal to Experience: Self-Identity, Late Modernity, and the Politics of Immediacy.* Montreal: McGill-Queen's University Press.

Izenberg, Gerald (1992). *Impossible Individuality: Romanticism, Revolution, and the Origins of Modern Selfhood, 1787–1802.* Ewing: Princeton University Press.

Jannidis, Fotis (1996). "'Individuum est ineffabile'. Zur Veränderung der Individualitätssemantik im 18. Jahrhundert und ihrer Auswirkung auf die Figurenkonzeption im Roman" ["'Individual est ineffabile'. On the Change of Semantics of Individuality in the 18th Century and its Impact on the Conception of Characters in the Novel"]. *Aufklärung* 9 (2): 77-110.

Janjion, Marija (1976). *Romantizam. Revolucija. Marksizam* [*Romanticism, Revolution, Marxism*]. Beograd: Nolit.

Jetten, Jolanda, Tom Postmes & Brendan J. Mcauliffe (2002). "'We're all Individuals': Group Norms of Individualism and Collectivism, Levels of Identification and Identity Threat." *European Journal of Social Psychology* 32: 189–207.

Kant, Immanuel (1968 [1784]). "Beantwortung der Frage: Was ist Aufklärung?" ["Answering the Question: What is Enlightenment?"] In *Kants gesammelten Schriften*, vol. 8. Berlin: de Gruyter, pp. 35–42.

Kemper, Dirk (2004). *Ineffabile. Goethe und die Individualitätsproblematik der Moderne* [*Ineffabile. Goethe and the Modernity's Problem of Individuality*]. München: Wilhelm Fink.

Kippenberg, Hans G., Yme B. Kuiper, Andy F. Sanders (Eds.) (1990). *Concepts of Person in Religion and Thought.* Berlin: de Gruyter.

Lecourt, Dominique (2004). „On Individualism." *Angelaki* 9 (3): 11–15.

Leibniz, Gottfried Wilhelm (1982). *New Essays on Human Understanding.* Cambridge: Cambridge University Press.

Locke, John (1823 [1689]). *Two Treatises of Government*. The Works of John Locke, vol. 5. London: Thomas Tegg, http://www.yorku.ca/comninel/courses/3025pdf/Locke.pdf (Accessed 9 Feb. 2014).

Luhmann, Niklas (1986). *Love as Passion: The Codification of Intimacy*. Cambridge: Harvard University Press.

Lukes, Steven (1973). *Individualism*. New York: Harper & Row.

Macpherson, C. B. (1962). *The Political Theory of Possessive Individualism: Hobbes to Locke*. Oxford: Oxford University Press.

Maistre, Joseph de (1996 [1796]). *Against Rousseau: "On the State of Nature" and "On the Sovereignty of the People"*. Ed. Richard Lebrun. Montreal: McGill-Queen's University Press.

Maistre, Joseph de (2012). "Study on Sovereignty." In *The Generative Principle of Political Constitutions: Studie on Sovereignty, Religion, and Enlightenment*. New Brunswick: Transaction, pp. 93-129.

Macintyre, Alasdair (1998). *A Short History of Ethics: A History of Moral Philosophy from the Homeric Age to the Twentieth Century*. 2nd ed. New York: Routledge.

Macintyre, Alasdair (2007). *After Virtue: A Study in Moral Theory*. 3rd ed. Notre Dame: University of Notre Dame Press.

Martin, Luther H. (1994). "The Anti-Individualistic Ideology of Hellenistic Culture." *Numen* 41 (2): 117-140.

Mauss, Marcel (1985 [1938]). "A Category of the Human Mind: The Notion of Person; The Notion of Self." In *The Category of the Person: Anthropology, Philosophy, History*. Eds. Michael Carrithers, Steven Collins & Steven Lukes. Cambridge: Cambridge University Press, pp. 1-25.

Mayordomo, Moisés (2011). "The Bright Side of Jesus, oder Einführung in die Brianologie. Wirkungsgeschichtliche und theologische Annäherungen an 'Monty Python's Life of Brian.'" ["The Bright Side of Jesus, or Introduction to Brianology. Historical and Theological Approaches to 'Monty Python's Life of Brian'"] In *Imagination in der Praktischen Theologie. Festschrift für Maurice Baumann* [*Imagination in Practical Theology. Festschrift for Maurice Baumann*]. Eds. David

Plüss, Johannes Stückelberger & Andreas Kessler. Zürich: Theologischer Verlag, pp. 53-66.

Meinecke, Friedrich (1957). *Die Idee der Staatsräson in der neueren Geschichte* [*The Idea of the Raison d'etat in Recent History*]. Werke, vol. 1. Munich: R. Oldenbourg.

Meinecke, Friedrich (1965 [1936]). *Die Entstehung des Historismus* [*Historism: The Rise of a New Historical Outlook*]. Werke, vol. 3, München: R. Oldenbourg.

Mill, John Stuart (2001 [1859]). *On Liberty*. Kitchener: Batoche Books.

Morris, Colin (1972). *The Discovery of the Individual 1050-1200*. New York: Harper.

Müller, Adam (2006 [1809]). *Die Elemente der Staatskunst* [*The Elements of Statesmanship*], vol. 1. Hildesheim: Olms.

Nassar, Dalia (2013). *The Romantic Absolute: Being and Knowing in Early German Romantic Philosophy, 1795-1804*. Chicago: University of Chicago Press.

Nohl, Hermann (1970). *Die deutsche Bewegung. Vorlesungen und Aufsätze zur Geistesgeschichte 1770-1830* [*The German Movement. Lectures and Essays on Intellectual History 1770-1830*]. Eds. Otto Friedrich Bollnow & Frithjof Rodi. Göttingen: Vandenhoek & Ruprecht.

Oergel, Maike (2006). *Culture and Identity: Historicity in German Literature and Thought 1770–1815*. Berlin: de Gruyter.

Pateman, Carole (1988). *The Sexual Contract*. Stanford: Stanford University Press.

Pelling, Christopher (1990). "Introduction." In *Characterization and Individuality in Greek Literature*. Ed. Christopher Pelling. Oxford: Clarendon, pp. i-vii.

Plessner, Helmuth (1950). *Lachen und Weinen: eine Untersuchung nach den Grenzen menschlichen Verhaltens* [*Laughing and Crying. A Study of the Limits of Human Behaviour*]. Bern: A. Francke.

Schilbrack, Kevin (2006). "'Life's a Piece of Shit': Heresy, Humanism, and Heroism in Monty Python's Life of Brian." In *Monty Python and Philosophy: Nudge Nudge, Think Think!* Eds. Gary L. Hardcastle & George A. Reisch. Chicato: Open Court, pp. 13-23.

Schlegel, Friedrich von (1964 [1800-1801]). *Jenaer Vorlesungen zur Tranzendentalphilosophie* [*Jenaer Lectures on the Tranzendental Philosophy*]. Kritische Friedrich Schlegel Ausgabe, vol. 12. München: F. Schöningh.

Simmel, Georg (1950). "Fundamental Problems of Sociology (Individual and Society)." In *The Sociology of Georg Simmel*. Ed. K. H. Wolff. New York: The Free Press, pp. 1–84.

Snell, Bruno (1982). *The Discovery of the Mind: The Greek Origins of European Thought*. New York: Dover.

Talmon, Jacob (1952). *The Origins of Totalitarian Democracy*. London: Seeker and Warburg.

Talmon, Jacob (1959). "Utopianism and Politics: A Conservative View." *Commentary*, August: 49-54. https://www.commentarymagazine.com/articles/utopianism-and-politicsa-conservative-view/ (Accessed 2 Apr. 2015).

Tarn, W. W. (1961). *Hellenistic Civilisation*. Cleveland: Meridian.

Taylor, Charles (2006). *Sources of the Self: The Making of the Modern Identity*, 8th ed. Cambridge: Cambridge University Press.

Tocqueville, Alexis de (1900). *Democracy in America*. London: The Colonial Press. https://babel.hathitrust.org/cgi/pt?id=nyp.33433081795258;view=1up;seq=11 (Accessed 11 July 2012).

Tracy, Antoine Louis Claude, Comte Destutt de (1970 [1817]). *A Treatise on Political Economy*. Ed. Thomas Jefferson. New York: Augustus M. Kelly.

Trilling, Lionel (1972). *Sincerity and Authenticity*. London: Oxford University Press.

Vintaloro, Giordano (2008). *"Non sono il Messia, lo giuro su Dio!"* – *Messianismo e modernità in Life of Brian dei Monty Python* [*"I am not the Messiah, I swear to God! " – Messianism and Modernity in Monty Python's Life of Brian*]. Trieste: Battello Stampatore.

Woolf, Leonard (1931). *After the Deluge: A Study in Communal Psychology*. London: Hogarth. http://natlib.govt.nz/records/21970480?search%5Bi%5D%5Bcategory%5D=Books&search%5Bpath%5D=items&search%5Btext%5D=Deluge (Accessed 4 Dec. 2016).

CONTENTS OF EARLIER VOLUMES

Advances in Sociology Research. Volume 25

Advances in Sociology Research. Volume 24

INDEX

D

E

H

I

N

S